ISAIAH

"THE SALVATION OF
JEHOVAH"

ISAIAH

"THE SALVATION OF JEHOVAH"

*A Survey of the Book of Isaiah
the Prophet*

by

ALFRED MARTIN, Th.D.

MOODY PRESS
CHICAGO

Copyright © 1956, by
THE MOODY BIBLE INSTITUTE
OF CHICAGO

ISBN: 0-8024-2023-0

27 29 30 28 26

Printed in the United States of America

PREFACE

PERHAPS you have wanted to become better acquainted with the Bible but have hesitated to study a book like Isaiah because of its length or because of the newness and strangeness to you of much of its subject matter. This brief elementary survey of Isaiah is designed to be of some help to you in entering into the contents of that glorious book.

If you are looking for a technical verse-by-verse commentary on the Hebrew text of Isaiah, this is not the book for you. If you want a detailed analysis of the book, you must look elsewhere. This book does not claim to be an original work of scholarship, although accuracy has been sought, and indebtedness to many scholarly writers and teachers is freely and gladly acknowledged.

There has been no attempt at documentation, for that would defeat the intended purpose. This is a study in which the researches of many interpreters are translated into language that will mean something to the average student of the Bible who has not had a theological education. You will have to be the judge of how successfully this is done.

Too many students of the Bible get bogged down in details before they know enough about its broad general teachings. This leads to discouragement and defeat in

Bible study. A knowledge of the factual content of the
Bible is basic to its interpretation; yet some will quibble
over the exact meaning of a phrase or a word (which is
certainly of great importance) when they do not have
the slightest awareness of its relation to the meaning of
the book as a whole. This "can't-see-the-forest-for-the-
trees" approach is a detriment. One ought to take a good
look at the forest first; then in due time the trees will
stand out in all their beauty. This is, of course, what
Dr. James M. Gray said so many years ago in his *How
to Master the English Bible*.

Reading this book will not in itself give you an acquaintance with Isaiah. The way to know Isaiah is to
read *Isaiah*. This self-evident truth is nowhere more
neglected than in Bible study. Therefore if you are really
in earnest, you will read Isaiah through more than once
and you will use this brief survey as a guide or study-
help, not as an end in itself.

CONTENTS

CHAPTER 1

BACKGROUNDS

The Place of Isaiah in the Bible

THE ANCIENT HEBREWS spoke of the Sacred Books (which we call the Old Testament) as "The Law, The Prophets, and The Writings." The Lord Jesus Christ, in speaking to His disciples after His resurrection from the dead, referred to this threefold division (Luke 24:44).

The Prophets are those books which were written by men who held the office of prophet. A prophet was more than a foreteller of the future; he was an official spokesman for God. His message included warning, exhortation, encouragement, and comfort, as well as prediction. The prophet's message concerning the future was one of the proofs that his entire message came from God, who alone knows the end from the beginning (Isa. 46:10).

The Prophets were further classified as *The Former Prophets* and *The Latter Prophets*. The first of these sections was made up of books that are historical in content, but which nevertheless were written by official prophets. These are the books of Joshua, Judges, Samuel, and Kings (each of the last two being originally one book in the Hebrew Bible).

The Latter Prophets are Isaiah, Jeremiah, Ezekiel, and

9

The Twelve. This last title includes all the books from
Hosea through Malachi. At the head of these Latter
Prophets, although certainly not the earliest to be written, stands the incomparable Book of Isaiah. Its position
shows the importance which was attached to it from
ancient times.

The Writer of the Book

The Book of Isaiah receives its name (as do all the
books of the Latter Prophets) from its writer, Isaiah the
son of Amoz (1:1). Little is known of the man, yet more
than of most of the other prophets. Nothing is known
with certainty about his ancestry, although ancient Jewish tradition says that he was related to the royal family
of Judah. His father must not be confused with the
prophet Amos; these are two entirely different names
and have no connection.

It is known that Isaiah lived in the city of Jerusalem,
that he was married (8:3), and that he had at least two
sons (7:3; 8:3). His ministry continued during the reigns
of four kings of Judah—Uzziah, Jotham, Ahaz, and Hezekiah—although he did not begin his work until almost
the end of Uzziah's reign. He must have had a ministry
of about forty years. While Old Testament chronology
is a difficult subject at best, and there is much difference
of opinion about dates, it can be asserted that Isaiah
prophesied during the latter half of the eighth century
before Christ. He himself tells us that he saw the Lord
in the year that King Uzziah died, which may have been
740 B.C. He was prophesying at the time the Northern
Kingdom of Israel was taken into captivity by the Assyrians in 722 B.C., and undoubtedly continued for some

years after that. Hezekiah, the last of the four kings during whose reigns he ministered, probably died in 686
B.C.

Ancient tradition maintains that Isaiah was put to
death by Hezekiah's son and successor, the wicked Manas-
seh, even telling us that he was killed by being "sawn
asunder." Some have thought that the allusion to this
dreadful form of martyrdom in Hebrews 11:37 is a reference to Isaiah, but of course we have no way of knowing.

Other Prophets in Isaiah's Time

The prophet Amos either had brought or was bringing
his ministry to a close when Isaiah began to prophesy in
Judah. Amos, although a native of Judah, had been sent
by God to prophesy against the Northern Kingdom,
Israel. Hosea began his ministry in Israel sometime before Isaiah began his in Judah. Micah was a younger
contemporary, prophesying like Isaiah in Judah. There
are a number of similarities between their two books,
one passage in Isaiah 2 especially being parallel to a
passage in Micah 4.

The Historical Background of Isaiah

The historical background of Isaiah is found in II
Kings and II Chronicles. For about two centuries the
kingdom had been divided. Israel, the Northern Kingdom, was ruled by a succession of evil kings from a number of different ruling families or dynasties, all of whom
followed in the footsteps of the first king, Jeroboam the
son of Nebat, "who made Israel to sin." Not one of the

kings of Israel—not even Jehu, who had wiped out the
Sidonian Baal worship imported into Israel by Jezebel—
had disclaimed the wicked practice of Jeroboam in setting up idols at Dan and Bethel and identifying them
with the God who had brought His people out of Egypt
(I Kings 12:26-30).

In the period just before Isaiah began his ministry, the
kingdom of Israel was ruled for forty-one years by the
powerful and brilliant Jeroboam II of the house of Jehu.
This was the time of the greatest outward prosperity and
enlargement of the Northern Kingdom, but it was rotten
at the core and was hastening toward the ultimate judgment of God, as Amos and Hosea showed.

The dominant world power in Isaiah's day was Assyria.
Before this time Egypt had been very important; now,
however, its power was ebbing, and it became involved
in a struggle to the death with the rising, aggressive
Assyria. One must know something of this in order to
understand the political allusions in Isaiah. During the
prophet's lifetime, the mighty Assyrian Kingdom swallowed up Israel and invaded his own country of Judah,
seriously threatening it.

Judah was ruled by the descendants of King David.
Some of these were wicked, some good. Even with pe-
riods of revival and reformation under godly kings, the
over-all spiritual tendency of Judah was downward.
Outward prosperity, especially in Uzziah's long reign,
caused the nation to forget God. Uzziah and his son
Jotham on the whole were good kings, in spite of Uzziah's
attempt late in life to intrude into the work of the priests
(II Kings 15:3, 34; II Chron. 26:16-21).

Jotham's son Ahaz was an evil man who introduced
abominable pagan practices into the kingdom (II Kings

16:2-4). At various times Judah sought alliances either
with Assyria or with Egypt. Isaiah denounced these alliances and called upon the nation to turn back to God.
In the distance loomed the Babylonian captivity, the
theme of much of Isaiah's prophecy, although the new
Babylonian Empire had not become powerful in Isaiah's
day and did not threaten Judah until a century later,
in the time of King Josiah and the prophet Jeremiah.

In spite of the downward spiritual trend there was
revival in Judah for a time under Hezekiah, one of the
best and most remarkable of all the kings (II Kings
18:1-20; II Chron. 29:1—32:33). King Hezekiah and the
prophet Isaiah were great friends and compatriots in a
time of peril and apostasy.

The Unity of the Book of Isaiah

Since the year 1750 a great many destructive critics of
the Bible have denied or doubted the unity of the Book
of Isaiah, although there is no evidence whatever that
the book ever existed in a form different from that in
which we find it today. Uniform Hebrew and Christian
tradition has accepted the unity of this book for many
centuries. This is a fact which, as someone has said, cannot be overturned by a mere theory.

Beginning with only a chapter or a few chapters, critics
later became bolder in their destruction of the book, until they were willing to leave very little of it to the real
Isaiah. Toward the close of the nineteenth century it
became fashionable to speak of Isaiah and Deutero-Isaiah
(II Isaiah), with the claim that the latter part of the
book (ch. 40-66) could not have been written by Isaiah
in the eighth century B.C., but must have been written by

some unknown prophet in Babylon, who dreamed of the
return of his people from their captivity.

One reason for the theory of the Deutero-Isaiah is
that many scholars who studied the Bible were infected
with the virus of rationalism. They did not believe in
miracles or in genuine prophecy. When a book of the
Bible contains a specific prediction, the most common
explanation given by people of this type is that it is not
really a prediction, but must have been written at a later
time than commonly supposed, in the period of the pre-
dicted event or afterward. Isaiah contains some very specific predictive prophecies. One of the noteworthy ones
is the mention by name of Cyrus, the Persian king, in
chapters 44 and 45. A rationalistic critic would not admit
that Isaiah could have named Cyrus two centuries before
Cyrus lived.

The basic issue is the inspiration of the Bible. If the
Bible were merely a human book like other books, then
Isaiah's mention of Cyrus would be unbelievable. But if
the Bible is the verbally inspired, inerrant Word of God,
then such mention is not unbelievable. In reality the
issue is not between the doubter and Isaiah alone or
between the doubter and the believer, but between the
doubter and the New Testament, or fundamentally between the doubter and the Lord Jesus Christ.

Most rationalistic students of the Bible have not been
content to have even two Isaiahs. There is a theory of
a Trito-Isaiah (III Isaiah) , who is supposed to have written the bulk of the material in chapters 55 through 66.
This writer is placed as late as the fifth century B.C., in
the land of Israel after the captivity. Still other theories
call for a multitude of different writers and redactors or

editors who have had a hand in the book which we now have.

The attempts to dissect the Book of Isaiah, similar to the various documentary theories of the books of Moses, have not a shred of real evidence, but are based, as has been said, upon a denial of authentic prophecy and upon the mere conjectures or imaginings of the critics.

The Book of Isaiah gives evidence of being a unity. It was the custom of the Latter Prophets to head their writings with their own name. There is only one name attached to this book, the name of Isaiah the son of Amoz. The New Testament writers quote from all parts of the book and consistently refer to it as the work of Isaiah. In John 12:38-41 passages are quoted from Isaiah 53 and Isaiah 6 and are attributed to the same writer.

In addition to the uniform tradition, the claim of the book itself to be a unity, and the testimony of the New Testament, there are evidences within the book itself, such as the literary style and the repetition of leading expressions or motifs. Throughout the book, for example, God is referred to as "the Holy One of Israel." This title, found twenty-five times in Isaiah, is used only six times in all the rest of the Old Testament, and one of those times is in II Kings 19, which is identical to Isaiah 37.

Extensive proof of the unity of Isaiah must be left to the works of Old Testament introduction, the technical commentaries, and other specialized writings. The present treatment is based upon an unshaken faith in that unity.

CHAPTER 2

A GENERAL LOOK

Isaiah, the Prophet of the Gospel

No book of the Old Testament except Psalms is quoted or referred to in the New Testament as often as Isaiah. While the prophet had much to say to his own time, and was concerned largely with the coming Babylonian captivity and its aftermath, he was distinctively the evangelical prophet, the prophet of the Gospel. His book abounds in Messianic allusions. If we do not see the Lord Jesus Christ in the pages of Isaiah, we are very blind indeed.

In later chapters we shall speak more particularly of some of the prophecies of Christ. At present, in order to create an impression of the Messianic content of the book, we need only mention that this is the book of the virgin-born Immanuel (7:14); of the Child born and Son given, whose name is "Wonderful, Counselor, The mighty God, The everlasting Father, The Prince of Peace" (9:6); of the Branch from the roots of Jesse (11:1); of the King who shall "reign in righteousness" (32:1); of the One who feeds "his flock like a shepherd" (40:11); of the Servant in whom God finds His delight (42:1); of the "man of sorrows" and the "lamb" brought to the slaughter (53:3, 7). All these and many more

16

are vivid pictures of the Lord Jesus Christ, written down by inspiration seven hundred years before His coming into the world.

As we look through the New Testament, we see in many places the name of Isaiah ("Esaias" in the Authorized Version, from the Greek spelling of the name). Matthew quotes Isaiah repeatedly to show that Jesus of Nazareth is the promised Messiah and King (Matt. 4:14; 8:17; 12:17). John the Baptizer, beginning his mighty ministry, quotes Isaiah (John 1:23). The Lord Jesus Himself, in the synagogue at Nazareth, "where he had been brought up," reads from the Book of Isaiah and announces the fulfillment of the prophecy which He has read (Luke 4:16-21). The apostle John reports that Isaiah spoke of the glory of the Lord Jesus (John 12:41). The Ethiopian treasurer, returning home from his trip to Jerusalem, is reading Isaiah (Acts 8:28). Paul, in both his oral and his written ministry, quotes Isaiah (Acts 28:25-27; Rom. 9:27, 29; 10:16, 20; 15:12).

References to Isaiah in the New Testament are not limited to those places in which his name is actually mentioned. Often he is quoted as "a prophet" or "the prophet," and often brief allusions are made to some phrase in his book without a formal quotation.

The Theme of the Book

Certainly in the overruling providence of God it is no accident that this particular prophet had this particular name. *Isaiah* means "the salvation of Jehovah," and there could be no more fitting statement of the theme of the book. The prophet must, in conformity with his God-appointed mission, proclaim judgment for sin, must

announce the coming Babylonian captivity; but even
amid those passages which speak of captivity, there are
gleams of deliverance; and eventually this deliverance
becomes the substance of a great and exultant strain of
prophecy. This cannot be limited to the deliverance
from Babylon under Cyrus, prominent as that is in the
prophecy. No, a far greater deliverance is in view—deliverance by Immanuel; the extension of Jehovah's salvation, through His Servant, to the "ends of the earth";
the world-wide rule of the Messiah in righteousness and
peace. The scope of Isaiah's "vision" (1:1) is as broad
as the whole world and reaches on into the millennial
kingdom of Christ, and beyond that to the new heavens
and the new earth (66:22). With such a theme, who
could not sing? And when the singer is Isaiah, borne
along by the Spirit of God (II Peter 1:21), small wonder
that the song is one of exceptional beauty and power.

The Style of the Book

True, the Book of Isaiah is not a song in the strictest
sense of the term. Nevertheless, large portions of it are
poetic, more than is generally realized. In extent and
variety of vocabulary Isaiah excels; this is occasioned, no
doubt, by the length of the book and by its unusual
variety in subject matter. Figures of speech abound.
Personification, metaphor, simile follow one another in
rapid succession. There is paronomasia, or play on
words, which is not usually evident in the English translation. Alliteration, also lost in translation, is prominent;
and the use of a refrain is a frequent literary device which
can be carried over into the English.

There are actual songs in the book, such as the song of the vineyard (ch. 5) ; the song of the coming salvation (ch. 12) ; the song of the rejoicing desert (ch. 35) ; the song of the restored wife (ch. 54) ; and many others.

Another characteristic mark of Isaiah's style is his use of satire. Where could one find a more scathing denunciation of idolatry than in Isaiah's mocking comment about the man who cuts down a tree, uses part of it to make a fire to warm himself and to cook his food, and makes another part of it into a god (44:13-20) ?

Arrangement of the Prophecies

It was customary for the Old Testament prophets to deliver their messages orally before committing them to writing. In a long ministry such as Isaiah had, it is obvious that he gave more messages than are written in this book. Not only the oral messages, but also the written form that is preserved, and in fact, the way in which the prophecies are arranged are from God.

There are few dates given in the book, but from these few it appears that the prophecies are arranged in chronological order. Isaiah tells us in the beginning that he prophesied during the reigns of four kings of Judah: Uzziah, Jotham, Ahaz, and Hezekiah (1:1). The first note of time is the reference to the year of King Uzziah's death (6:1), and that is followed almost immediately by mention of the "days of Ahaz" (7:1). Consequently we assume that the prophecies in the first six chapters were given during the reigns of Uzziah and Jotham. Part of Jotham's reign was during the lifetime of his father, for Uzziah had been smitten by God with leprosy for in-

truding into the priestly office, and had to be kept in
isolation during the last years of his life (II Chron. 26:
16-23).

The next date given is the year of the death of King
Ahaz (14:28). The only other time references are to an
Assyrian invasion in the time of Sargon (20:1) and to
the great Assyrian invasion of Judah in the fourteenth
year of the reign of King Hezekiah (36:1).

Basic Outline of the Book

The simplest, and probably the most logical, outline
of the Book of Isaiah is that which sees it in two main
divisions. Everyone recognizes that there is a difference
between these two parts, so much in fact, that destructive
critics—as we have seen—have disputed the unity of the
book. These critics, of course, have exaggerated the differences and ignored the similarities. There is, nevertheless, a marked change of tone at the beginning of
chapter 40.

An easy way to remember the divisions of Isaiah is to
recall that there are as many chapters in the first part of
the book as there are books in the Old Testament (39),
and as many chapters in the second part of the book as
there are books in the New Testament (27). One should
not look for any doctrinal significance in this, for the
chapter divisions which we have now were not in the
Bible originally.

Without any attempt to be original, one can say in a
general way that the first part of Isaiah has as its theme
judgment from God, and that the second part has as its
theme *comfort from God.* The dominant note in each
case is struck at the very beginning—God's ringing in-

dictment of the kingdom of Judah in chapter 1, where
the city of Jerusalem is actually called Sodom and Gomorrah (1:10); and God's call to speak comforting words to
Jerusalem after her severe trials, in chapter 40 (40:1, 2).

Analysis of the First Part of Isaiah

There is always a danger in Bible study of construct-
ing artificial and arbitrary outlines and superimposing
them upon the book being studied. It is hardly necessary
to say that this should be avoided. One ought to search
the book itself to see what the logical divisions are. It
has been stated that the book as a whole is in two main
parts. The next step is to discover what subdivisions
there are in the first part.

The first six chapters come to a climax with Isaiah's
account of his vision of the Lord, and are further set
apart by the time note at the beginning of chapter 7,
which introduces a later prophecy. In a similar way,
chapters 7 through 12 have a central theme, for the troubles in the time of Ahaz give occasion to the great prophecy of Immanuel and His coming kingdom. There is no
difficulty in recognizing a distinct section in chapters 13
through 23; here the unifying word is *burden,* a prophecy
of grievous import. Chapters 24 through 27 likewise
form a unity, describing events of the last days. The next
section is clearly defined by the use of the word *woe,*
and includes chapters 28 through 33. A brief section of
two chapters (34 and 35) follows, again leading up to
the Kingdom Age. The concluding section in this part
of the book tells of historical events in Hezekiah's reign
(ch. 36 through 39).

While no claim is made that this outline is inspired,

it seems like a logical grouping of the material, and it has
the advantage of being based largely upon clues in the
Scripture itself. Consequently we say that there are seven
sections in the first part of Isaiah.

Part One: The Judgment of God (1—39)
    I. Opening Prophecies (1—6)
    II. Prophecies of Immanuel (7—12)
    III. The Burdens (13—23)
    IV. Punishment and Kingdom Blessing (24—27)
    V. The Woes (28—33)
    VI. Indignation and Glory (34, 35)
    VII. Historical Interlude (36—39)

Analysis of the Second Part of Isaiah

In the second part of the book the prophet is allowed
to look beyond the Babylonian captivity to the return,
and to see that return as a foreshadowing of a greater
future deliverance through the Messiah. From this ideal
point of view, the prophet can see the captivity as past
(although literally it did not begin until about a century after Isaiah's lifetime) , and can rejoice in the glories
of Israel's restoration.

Many writers have observed that the second part of
Isaiah seems to be made up of twenty-seven brief sections,
corresponding in general to the present chapter divisions.
These are clearly grouped into three longer sections of
nine chapters each. This is not a commentator's arbitrary
or whimsical arrangement, for it is imbedded in the structure of the book itself. Twice in this part of the book
God makes the statement: "There is no peace . . . to the

wicked." This double utterance marks the threefold division of the second part of Isaiah (48:22; 57:21).

The symmetrical arrangement of the second part of Isaiah cannot be accidental. Further comment will be made later in the appropriate places concerning the inner structure of the three sections. Chapters 40 through 48 tell of the coming deliverance from Babylon and draw the contrast between the true God and idols. Chapters 49 through 57, forming the central section of this part of Isaiah, have as their main theme the two great lines of Messianic prophecy mentioned in the New Testament: "the sufferings of Christ and the glory that should follow" (I Peter 1:11). The last section, chapters 58 through 66, brings to a climax the teachings concerning God's purpose for Israel, the coming glory of His people.

We can, therefore, chart the second part of Isaiah in this way:

Part Two: The Comfort of God (40—66)

    I. Deliverance of God's People (40—48)

   II. The Suffering Servant as the Redeemer (49—57)

  III. The Glorious Consummation (58—66)

With this over-all view of the book, we are now ready to look more closely into its various sections.

OPENING PROPHECIES

T HE PROPHECIES in the first six chapters of Isaiah, delivered during the reigns of Uzziah and Jotham, show
the moral corruption of the people of Judah and their
continuing and increasing hardness of heart. It is in this
section that we see God's indictment of the nation and
learn of the prophet Isaiah's own commission. Here also,
almost at the beginning, we are permitted to see the
future kingdom of Christ. The section can be outlined
as follows:

Part One: The Judgment of God (1—39)

   I. Opening Prophecies (1—6)

      A. God's Lament over Judah's Corruption (1)

         1. Heading of the Whole Book (1:1)

         2. God's Indictment (1:2-23)

         3. God's Vengeance (1:24-31)

      B. The Kingdom and Its Introductory Judgments
         (2—4)

         1. Messiah's Reign (2:1-4)

         2. Appeal and Warning (2:5—3:26)

         3. The Branch of Jehovah (4:1-6)

      C. Judah's Sins and the Resultant Woes (5)

         1. The Song of the Vineyard (5:1-6)

         2. The Meaning of the Song (5:7-30)

D. Isaiah's Call and Commission (6)
  1. The Vision (6:1-4)
  2. Confession and Cleansing (6:5-7)
  3. The Prophet's Commission (6:8-13)

The Heading of the Book

The opening verse is really the divinely inspired title of the book. It is called the "vision" which Isaiah "saw." This indicates supernatural revelation. We do not know precisely how God gave the message to Isaiah, but the wording makes it plain that Isaiah did not originate that which follows; he "saw" it, that is, he received it by supernatural prophetic perception. He was one of those "holy men of God" who "spake as they were moved by the Holy Ghost" (II Peter 1:21).

The message concerns the Southern Kingdom primarily, and the capital city, Jerusalem, is singled out as being representative of the kingdom as a whole. When we realize that the kingdom of Judah was ruled by descendants of David and that the temple worship was located there, we can realize more clearly the awfulness of the apostasy and the force of the indictment which God brings against the nation.

God's Indictment

The call to the heavens and the earth to hear reminds one of Moses' prophetic song in Deuteronomy 32. In spite of all God's blessings upon His people, in spite of the special privileges which He has given them, these children have rebelled against Him. They are worse, far worse, than the ox and the ass, two domestic animals that

are noted for their stupidity and their stubbornness.
Their sin was not a passing thing, it was a habitual state.
Jehovah is here (v. 4) for the first time in the book char-
acterized as the "Holy One of Israel." As the Holy One
He could not but be provoked by the exceeding sinful-
ness of the people.

Yet throughout the accusation which God makes
against His people, the tone is one of lamentation and
pleading. God does not gloat over the distress of the
wicked. He rather wants the wicked to turn back unto
Himself. "Why," He pleads (v. 5), "why should ye be
stricken any more?" The conditions described in these
verses are a beginning of the fulfillment of the curses
pronounced upon Israel for disobedience, as recorded in
Leviticus 26 and Deuteronomy 28 and 29. While some
commentators take verse 7 and following to be a description of the prophet's own time, this does not seem prob-
able. He is allowed by God to look ahead to what will
be the end result of that moral corruption which is already so apparent. The judgment is viewed as if it had
already come, and we see the vineyard stripped bare,
with the very small remnant surviving (vv. 8, 9). God
does not bring utter destruction upon Judah as He did
upon Sodom and Gomorrah, although its sins were
enough to warrant it.

Indeed, God actually calls the nation Sodom and
Gomorrah (v. 10). No doubt many in Judah protested
that they did not deserve to be compared with those
wicked cities of the plain (described in Gen. 19). The
worst thing about their corruption, however, was that it
was covered with a cloak of religiosity. The people were
continually going through the forms and motions of
worship, following the outward requirements of the

Mosaic ritual which had been given by God Himself. But such sacrifices were meaningless, they were "vain oblations" (v. 13). The people were only wearing out the courts of the temple, for their sacrifices were not accompanied by the right attitude of heart toward God. The hands which they held up as suppliants toward God were stained with the blood of other men; they were oppressors and murderers (v. 15).

God is always gracious, merciful, and longsuffering. He appeals to these sinners, and that appeal is typical of His appeal to all sinners, today as well as in other days. How can they be made clean, as God requires them to be? He gives the answer Himself; He Himself furnishes the cleansing:

> Come now, and let us reason together, saith the LORD: though your sins be as scarlet, they shall be as white as snow; though they be red like crimson, they shall be as wool (v. 18).

From the teaching of the Bible as a whole we know that cleansing from sin is on the ground of the sacrifice of Christ, that sacrifice which is prophesied so graphically elsewhere in Isaiah. Israel could give no defense, but God extended grace to her. When grace is spurned, there can be nothing else but judgment.

The covenant relation of God with His people is often viewed in the Old Testament as a marriage. Here that city which had once been faithful to God is viewed as most unfaithful (v. 21). The former glories had been swallowed up in the general corruption and oppression.

God's Vengeance

When God announces His vengeance, He uses a com-

bination of names for Himself not found elsewhere in
the book (v. 24). First He calls Himself "the Lord,"
a word which means sovereign Master. Next He is
"Jehovah of hosts," the covenant-keeping God who con-
trols the armies of Heaven (the word *LORD* in the English Authorized Version denotes the Hebrew form
Jehovah). He is also "the mighty One of Israel." These
three names together, emphasizing the omnipotence of
God, show the certainty of the judgment which He will
bring to pass.

But judgment actually implies redemption for some,
for in the smelting process which is described (v. 25)
the good part will be left.

Reign of the Messiah

The prophecy now turns to Messianic times, for that
is always the significance of the expression, "the last
days" (2:2), in the Old Testament. These opening
verses of chapter 2 are almost the same as the opening
verses of Micah 4. Micah and Isaiah were contemporaries,
but it is not necessary to postulate the dependence of
one upon the other. God could give the same prophecy
to both men. This is a poetic description of the coming
earthly kingdom of the Lord Jesus Christ. One should
compare with it not only the parallel passage in Micah,
but also such other passages as Psalms 2 and 46.

Men yearn for peace, but they will not acknowledge
the hopelessness of their own efforts to achieve it. It is
only when the word of the Lord goes forth from Jerusalem (v. 3), when He Himself is reigning over the
nations, that lasting peace will come (v. 4). Disarma-
ment would be a foolish procedure now for peace-loving

nations, because of the presence of greed and aggression
in the world. When Christ reigns, there can be dis-
armament because He will enforce righteousness in the
earth.

Appeal and Warning

It is clear that the kingdom cannot be set up before
a time of judgment. Hence this passage of appeal and
warning is pertinent. There is undoubtedly in the passage a mingling of conditions in the prophet's own day
with conditions that will prevail in a future day of judgment, the "day of Jehovah" (v. 12). The idolatry which
had been the curse of Israel through multiplied genera-
tions is to be completely abolished (v. 18). Many of
the things mentioned in chapter 3 took place in the
capture of Jerusalem by the Babylonians; the repeated
reference to "that day," however, looks forward to Messianic times. The close of the chapter speaks of the
great depletion of the male population through warfare.
The first verse of chapter 4 really belongs with the end of
chapter 3. The women will be willing to give up their
rights which they could claim under the law (Exod. 21:
10) in order to have husbands.

The "Branch of Jehovah"

The "branch of Jehovah" mentioned in 4:2 can be no
other than the Messiah (cf. Jer. 23:5; 33:15; Zech. 3:8;
6:12). The mark of distinction in "that day" will not
be position or prestige, but holiness (v. 3). In beautiful
poetic language the Lord shows how His presence will
abide with His people (v. 5), as He abode with them in

earlier times during their wilderness journeys. It is remarkable how many times in the Book of Isaiah the
same sequence of events is covered, the events connected
with the future judgment of Israel and the Kingdom
Age when the Lord Jesus Christ will reign over the earth.

The Song of the Vineyard with Its Explanation

This is the announcement of judgment in the form
of a parable. Its presentation as a song may serve to
soften the harshness of the prophecy. It shows the fa-
vored position which Israel enjoyed; there can be no
question about the interpretation, because it is given in
the passage itself (v. 7). This is not the only place in
the Old Testament where Israel is compared with a
vineyard (cf. Ps. 80 and Hos. 10). The Lord Jesus undoubtedly alluded to this portion of Isaiah when He
gave His parable of the vineyard (Matt. 21:33-44), which
the chief priests and the Pharisees clearly perceived to be
directed against themselves.

Since God had planted this vineyard, He had a right
to expect good results from it. Instead of justice, however, He found oppression; instead of righteousness, the
cry of the oppressed (v. 7). The last clause of verse 7 is
an interesting example of paronomasia: the Hebrew
words for "righteousness" and "cry" sound very much
alike.

Some of the sins of Israel which bring this judgment
are then plainly enumerated. Grasping greediness will
be punished by barren fields, extensive crop failures
(vv. 8-10). Drunkenness will be punished with captivity
(vv. 11-14). God will see to it that men shall be brought
down and He Himself shall be exalted (vv. 15-17).

Woe is next pronounced against those who are defiant and rebellious (vv. 18, 19) ; against those who confuse moral issues (v. 20), a sin which is as prevalent in our day as in Isaiah's; against those who in their conceit depend upon their own faulty human wisdom (v. 21) ; against the drunken judges (vv. 22, 23).

God's justice will surely intervene. It is invoked first in a general statement (v. 24), then it is pictured as a blow from His hand (v. 25). Finally, it is seen as an invading army (vv. 26-30).

This section is thus at a close except for the record of the prophet's own commission in chapter 6. Throughout these chapters God's justice has been vindicated in the punishment of His people for their iniquity, for their iniquity has been fully revealed in all its hideousness. Yet, as has been seen, God's grace is still available. The stretched-out hand of threatening judgment is accompanied by the loving appeal to the individual who will turn to God.

CHAPTER 4

THE PROPHET'S COMMISSION

IN THIS ELEMENTARY SURVEY of Isaiah it is both necessary and desirable to give more attention to some parts of the book than to others. It is especially desirable that we see the prophecies of the Lord Jesus Christ in the book. While the sixth chapter is not a prophecy of Christ, it nevertheless has a direct connection with Him, as the New Testament shows:

> Therefore they could not believe, because that Esaias [Isaiah] said again, He hath blinded their eyes, and hardened their heart; that they should not see with their eyes, nor understand with their heart, and be converted, and I should heal them. These things said Esaias, when he saw his glory, and spake of him (John 12:39-41).

The context indicates that the pronouns refer to the Lord Jesus Christ. Isaiah saw *His* glory and spoke of *Him*. This is, of course, in the chapter which we are now considering.

The Vision

Isaiah could never forget the experience which he describes here. He would never be in doubt about it; he would always remember when it occurred. He dates it: "In the year that king Uzziah died." Some have imagined that the death of the king, perhaps held in high esteem by the young Isaiah, made it possible for him to open his eyes to wider visions, to see the heavenly King. This is mere speculation, and does not coincide with the dating which the prophet uses. The expression, "the year that king Uzziah died," would indicate that the king was still living when this event took place. If Uzziah had already died, the prophecy would have been dated according to the reign of Jotham. While we accept the Bible as the verbally inspired Word of God and recognize the fact that every word has meaning, we must be careful not to draw false inferences, not to jump to false conclusions.

Isaiah saw the Lord. We have already seen that John refers to this experience as a view of Christ's glory. The Son of God is always the Revealer of God, before His incarnation as well as after:

> No man hath seen God at any time; the only begotten Son, which is in the bosom of the Father, he hath declared him (John 1:18).

The word which is used here for *Lord* (6:1) means the "sovereign Master." It is used again in verses 8 and 11. A different word—the name *Jehovah*—is used in verses 3, 5, and 12. The One whom Isaiah saw is the absolute Disposer of all events, the absolute Master of men. His majesty and glory are set forth, as so often in the Scripture, with a minimum of descriptive words, yet with a graphic power that causes us to see and to feel.

The seraphim are mentioned only here by name in the Bible. The word means literally, "burning ones." They are evidently angelic beings of a very high order, for they are about the throne of God and are engaged in continual praise of Him. They help to express to our

feeble powers of perception the intense holiness of God.
There is certainly an intimation here of the Trinity—
that mysterious but certain doctrine which is only ob-
scurely seen in the Old Testament and blazed forth
clearly in the New.   Why do the seraphim cry this
threefold cry instead of a twofold, or fourfold, or mani-
fold one? Because there are three and only three Persons in the Godhead, each of whom is the Holy One
(cf. John 17:11; Luke 1:35). Isaiah's whole prophecy
shows the effect of this vision of God. He could not
forget that God is holy. He uses the title, "the Holy One
of Israel," twenty-five times in the book.

Confession and Cleansing

A vision of God gives a man a clear view of himself.
It is always thus. The patriarch Job, pronounced by
God Himself a "perfect and an upright man" (Job 1:8;
2:3), when he saw God, realized his own worthlessness:

> I have heard of thee by the hearing of the ear : but now
> mine eye seeth thee. Wherefore I abhor myself, and repent
> in dust and ashes (Job 42:5, 6).

Daniel, a "man greatly beloved" (Dan. 10:11), was
overwhelmed by the vision of the glory of God (10:15-
17). John, the "disciple whom Jesus loved" (John 21:
20), when he saw the Lord Jesus Christ in glory on the
island of Patmos, "fell at his feet as dead" (Rev. 1:17).
Isaiah is no exception. "Woe is me!" he cries, "for I
am undone" (6:5).

> The Lord Jehovah reigns, His throne is built on high;
> The garments He assumes are light and majesty;
> His glories shine with beams so bright,
> No mortal eye can bear the sight.

And will this sovereign King of glory condescend;
And will He write His name, my Father and my Friend?
I love His name, I love His word;
Join all my powers to praise the Lord!"
                                        —ISAAC WATTS

God has not brought Isaiah into this experience merely to let him despair. Confession is the gateway to
cleansing; for when the prophet realizes his need, God
can meet that need. So many people never get to the
point where they will admit that there is anything wrong
with them. Consequently they never acknowledge the
need of the Saviour. Self-righteousness holds the blessed
Lord at arm's length. He came not "to call the righteous,
but sinners to repentance" (Matt. 9:13). Likewise in
our lives as believers we sometimes are barren and un-
fruitful, out of fellowship with our Lord because we do
not confess our sins. "If we confess our sins, he is faithful and just to forgive us our sins, and to cleanse us
from all unrighteousness" (I John 1:9).

The live coal from the altar is here the instrument of
cleansing. The altar is the place of sacrifice. The truth
for us in New Testament terminology is that all cleansing
is based upon the death of Christ.

The Prophet's Commission

There is a natural sequence here which could not be
otherwise. The "woe" of confession is followed by the
"lo" of cleansing, and that in turn by the "go" of commission. God does not want and will not use unclean
instruments in His service. Even under these favorable
circumstances He awaits the prophet's answer, so to
speak. "Whom shall I send, and who will go for us?"
(6:8).

Down through the ages that call is repeated. God calls to you and to me today: "Who will go . . . ?" He does not always have the same commission to give. We can be thankful that our commission will not be just like Isaiah's. For Isaiah was not to have an easy time. He was not to see great crowds flocking to the Lord. He was told before he began that the multitudes would not heed him and that judgment would have to come upon his people. But, thank God, there was to be a tithe (6:13); there would always be some who would believe. God always has His remnant, like the seven thousand in Elijah's day (I Kings 19:18). Hence Paul can rejoice, "Even so then at this present time also there is a remnant according to the election of grace" (Rom. 11:5).

CHAPTER 5

IMMANUEL—THE VIRGIN'S SON

IT IS CHARACTERISTIC of predictive prophecy that it often mingles different times together in one composite picture. The prophet must speak, of course, to his own time, in a way that can be understood by his contemporaries. Yet he is not confined to his own time or even to the immediate future, but the Spirit of God bears him along to distant times and realms. Especially does the Holy Spirit bring to the attention of the prophet's hearers the times of the Messiah, the promised Redeemer.

This section of Isaiah, chapters 7 through 12, is an excellent illustration of this principle. The prophecies were given during the reign of Ahaz (7:1), at a time when Syria and Israel were allied against Judah and the craven, paganized King Ahaz momentarily expected to be destroyed by these two enemy powers. Furthermore, the terrible power of the far mightier Assyria threatened on the horizon. God through his prophet promises deliverance from these enemies, but shows that the ultimate deliverance of His people can come only through the One whose name is Immanuel. In these chapters are some of the best-known prophecies of Christ. A simple outline of the section is as follows:

Part One: The Judgment of God (1—39)

    I. Opening Prophecies (1—6)

   II. The Book of Immanuel (7—12)

      A. The Birth of Immanuel (7:1-16)

         1. Occasion of the Prophecy (7:1—9)

         2. The Sign to the House of David (7:10-16)

      B. The Assyrian Invasion (7:18—8:22)

      C. The Davidic Kingdom and King (9:1-7)

      D. God's Stretched-out Hand of Judgment (9:8—
10:34)

      E. The Branch from Jesse's Root (11:1-16)

      F. The Song of Redemption (12:1-6)

The Birth of Immanuel

It was a mark of the degeneration among the people of Israel that one branch of them would form an alliance with a pagan nation against the other. This was not the first time for such a sordid occurrence, but we can imagine the consternation in the corrupt court of Ahaz when the word came, "Syria is confederate with Ephraim" (7:2). The term *Ephraim* is often used in the prophets for the Northern Kingdom because of the leading place that the tribe of Ephraim exercised in it.

In the midst of the universal terror the prophet of God sturdily went forth at God's command to meet the king, taking with him, also by divine appointment, his son with a symbolic name—Shear-jashub, "a remnant shall return" (7:3). Amid human confusion there is divine assurance and stability:

> Thus saith the Lord GOD, It shall not stand, neither shall it come to pass (7:7).

Then, to reinforce the flat statement of deliverance, God invites the king to ask for a sign. Ahaz, whose character is well known from II Kings 16:2-4, with a pretense of piety sanctimoniously protested that he would not tempt the Lord. The historical record tells us that Ahaz, far from depending upon God, was even then seeking the help of Assyria to defeat his more immediate enemies. This was like a mouse sending for the cat to help him against two rats!

Passages such as this are the test of whether one really accepts the Bible as the Word of God or not. Liberal interpretation wallows in a quagmire of immediacy. It cannot or will not admit that God can blend together a near and a far view. It must seek the complete explanation of the passage in the prophet's own day, and that in the face of the fact that the New Testament plainly declares otherwise.

In spite of rationalistic denials and evasions, Isaiah 7:14 is a direct prophecy of the virgin birth of the Lord Jesus Christ. The quotation of it in Matthew 1:23 settles the question. Objection is raised that this could not be a sign to Ahaz, since the fulfillment did not come until long after his day. But the statement was made not merely to the individual, Ahaz, but to the "house of David," which Ahaz represented, no matter how poorly, in his generation. There is no need to see in this prophecy two children, one born at that time by natural processes and the other the virgin-born Son. Exhaustive studies of Robert Dick Wilson and others have shown that the Hebrew word is properly translated "virgin"; certainly the Greek word in Matthew 1:23, which is a quotation of this verse from Isaiah, can be translated in no other way.

There is, of course, contingency in the prophecy. The thought of verse 16 seems to be that if the baby Immanuel were born in the immediate future, before He would be old enough to make known His distinction between good and evil, the two enemy kings would withdraw. There is, therefore, both a message for the age and a message for the ages. Ahaz has the assurance that the Syrio-Israelitic invasion will not prevail; the house of David has the greater assurance of the great Deliverer, Immanuel.

This great prophetic name of the Lord Jesus Christ— "God with us"—sets forth both His deity and His humanity. This is what John had in mind when he said:

> And the Word was made flesh, and dwelt among us, (and we beheld his glory, the glory as of the only begotten of the Father,) full of grace and truth (John 1:14).

The same truth is revealed in a parallel passage to this in the ninth chapter of Isaiah. In connection with these prophecies one should read the passage on the Person of Christ in Philippians 2:5-11.

The Assyrian Invasion

The prophet goes on to show that Assyria will come in a more devastating invasion than that of Syria and Israel (7:20). As a symbol of this coming judgment Isaiah is instructed to name his second son Maher-shalal-hash-baz, "Haste ye, haste ye to the spoil" (8:1, 3). No matter how great a confederation of enemies there will be, however, God will deliver Judah if they will look to Him. They are to stand in reverential fear before Him rather than in terror of any adversaries:

> Sanctify the LORD of hosts himself; and let him be your
> fear, and let him be your dread (8:13).

Against those false teachers who would turn the people
to idolatrous and abominable spiritism, Isaiah exhorts
them to seek unto God. He alone can bring deliverance.

The Davidic Kingdom and King

Here again a tremendous leap is made across the centuries. In fact, two leaps are made. We are informed
in the New Testament that the prophecy is partially
fulfilled in the ministry of the Lord Jesus Christ in
Galilee at His first advent (cf. 9:1, 2 with Matt. 4:13-16).
Nevertheless it must be acknowledged that here as elsewhere the two comings of Christ are brought together
in one prophecy. Indeed, from the Old Testament alone
it could not be clearly seen that there were to be *two*
comings. That is a New Testament amplification. Peter
tells of the bewilderment of the Old Testament prophets:

> Of which salvation the prophets have inquired and
> searched diligently, who prophesied of the grace that should
> come unto you: searching what, or what manner of time
> the Spirit of Christ which was in them did signify, when
> it [he] testified beforehand the sufferings of Christ, and the
> glory that should follow (I Peter 1:10,11).

The birth of the child prophesied in Isaiah 9:6 has
taken place long ago, at Christ's first coming; His universal reign has not yet been fulfilled. That awaits His
return. Here, as has been noted, are the two natures
of Christ in one Person. "A child is born"—that is His
perfect humanity. "A son is given"—that is His absolute
deity. Lest there be any doubt of this fact, the prophecy
gives Him titles which no mere man could have: "Won-

derful, Counselor, The mighty God, The everlasting
Father, The Prince of Peace."

In a day when men are praised too much, even among
Christians, we need to praise Him who alone is worthy
of praise. It is easy to exaggerate in our estimation of
men; no one could ever exaggerate the worth of Jesus
Christ. He is "Wonderful" in His unique Person and in
His unique atoning work. No one else is the God-Man;
no one else could die for our sins, or even help Him to
do so:

> When he had by himself purged our sins, sat down on the
> right hand of the Majesty on high (Heb. 1:3).

In Jesus Christ are "hid all the treasures of wisdom
and knowledge" (Col. 2:3). No wonder that His name
is "Counselor." His almighty power, manifested in Creation and available to us, is seen in His title, "The
mighty God." He is "The Father of eternity," the One
who nourishes and protects His own forever. He is the
"Prince of Peace," the One who brings peace to the individual and who will ultimately bring peace to the
world. His kingdom with its resultant peace will continue (9:7). In order to show the certainty of this the
statement is made, "The zeal of the LORD of hosts will
perform this," a statement which occurs only in two
other places (Isa. 37:32; II Kings 19:31).

God's Stretched-Out Hand of Judgment

The stretched-out hand of God as seen repeatedly in
this section (9:12, 17, 21; 10:4; cf. also 5:25) is not in
this instance a display of mercy, but instead, an indication of judgment. God's previous judgments have not

had the desired effect of turning His people to repentance
(9:13) ; therefore He must continue to smite them.

We find then a paradoxical fact, referred to in other
connections in the Scripture. God is actually using the
wicked nation of Assyria to punish His own people
(10:5). "Surely the wrath of man shall praise thee"
(Ps. 76:10).

God will not allow Assyria to escape His righteous
judgment. How men delude themselves into thinking
that they are going their own way, declaring their in-
dependence of God! Assyria, that mighty nation, is serv-
ing a divine purpose as a tool in the Lord's hand. This
does not excuse Assyria's actions or absolve it of its guilt:

> Wherefore it shall come to pass, that when the Lord hath
> performed his whole work upon mount Zion and on Jeru-
> salem, I will punish the fruit of the stout heart of the king
> of Assyria, and the glory of his high looks (10:12).

God's sovereignty and man's responsibility are always
in perfect balance in the Word of God. Even though we
are not able to reconcile these paradoxical facts, we can
believe both because the Bible teaches both. God is sovereign in His universe; and at the same time man is
fully accountable to God for all his acts.

The reference to "that day" (v. 20) seems to carry the
prophecy over from the historical invasion in the prophet's own time to another tremendous invasion of the
land in the end-time. Whatever the exact connection may
be, the sequel in chapter 11 would seem to indicate such
a far view.

The Branch from Jesse's Root

How exquisitely the Lord Jesus Christ is portrayed in
these messages of the evangelical prophet! Here (11:1)

He is characterized again as the "Branch," although the Hebrew word here is not the same as in 4:2. He is seen as the true successor of David, the Messiah-King. The description of His endowment by the Spirit of God (v. 2) recalls that "God giveth not the Spirit by measure unto him" (John 3:34). His kingdom has been seen in a previous passage (9:7) as bringing peace; here the emphasis is upon the righteousness which will characterize it. Men are always looking for peace, but are not ready for a peace that will be based upon righteousness. No ordinary man, no matter how good his intentions may be, could possibly reign in perfect righteousness. Only the all-knowing, all-wise, all-holy Son of God can reign in righteousness (cf. 32:1).

Many are disposed to allegorize or spiritualize the Old Testament prophecies concerning the kingdom. Fulfilled prophecy, however, furnishes us a standard by which to interpret prophecy yet unfulfilled. If the prophecies concerning the sufferings of Christ were fulfilled in general in a literal manner, ought we not to expect the prophecies concerning His glory to be similarly fulfilled?

None can deny that there are many figures of speech in the prophetic passages; nor can God describe the coming glory for us in a way that we can understand completely. But if kingdom prophecy means anything, it means that there will come a day when Christ shall literally reign over this literal earth. This Messianic reign is often referred to as the Millennium, from the passage concerning the thousand years in Revelation 20 (the word *Millennium* is derived from Latin words meaning "a thousand years").

The New Testament tells us that eventually the material creation is to be delivered from the bondage into which it came because of man's sin (Rom. 8:19-22). This brief picture in Isaiah 11 shows us something of the coming glory of that day:

> They shall not hurt nor destroy in all my holy mountain:
> for the earth shall be full of the knowledge of the LORD,
> as the waters cover the sea (11:9).

The "highway" for the "remnant" of God's people finds an echo in later chapters of Isaiah (35:8; 40:3). This is an indication of a fact which every student of Isaiah should observe—the prophet's repeated use of themes or motifs, referred to earlier in our study.

The Song of Redemption

This lovely song, with which the section closes, expresses the praise and thanksgiving of the godly remnant of Israel in the coming day of salvation, "that day" (v. 1). It is in two parts (vv. 1, 2 and vv. 3-6). The first part looks back upon the judgment of God and then rests in His comfort (cf. 40:1). It acknowledges God as "strength," "song," and "salvation."

The second part is a pure hymn of praise, celebrating the "Holy One of Israel" in the midst of His people in Zion.

CHAPTER 6

BURDENS UPON THE NATIONS

As has been mentioned before, there are some parts of the Book of Isaiah which have a more direct bearing upon our lives than other parts. It is not intended in this brief survey to give an exposition of the whole book. Consequently we can pass rather lightly over the section containing chapters 13 through 23. This is not to say that these chapters are unimportant. It is simply to affirm that the purpose and desire of anyone using this study is to get an over-all picture of Isaiah and especially to see the teachings in the book concerning Christ.

This section contains messages to various Gentile nations. Each of the messages is called a "burden," a word which shows the nature of the prophecy. It is a message of weighty import, something heavy, in the sense that it produces sorrow or grief. These are prophecies of judgment. We can show the various messages thus:

Part One: The Judgment of God (1—39)

    I. Opening Prophecies (1—6)

   II. The Book of Immanuel (7—12)

 III. Burdens Upon the Nations (13—23)

       A. The Burden of Babylon (13:1—14:27)

       B. The Burden of Philistia (14:28-32)

       C. The Burden of Moab (15:1—16:14)

It can readily be seen that these prophecies are of unequal length and that some of them are difficult to identify even in regard to the nation to which they are addressed. Not all would agree that chapter 18 should be included in the burden of Egypt.

Only the veteran student of prophecy can link up these burdens with similar passages in other prophets, notably in Jeremiah and Ezekiel. It is not the intention of the present survey to make the study *burdensome.* There are, however, general principles which we can learn even from the most cursory acquaintance with chapters such as these. One such principle is God's absolute justice, the fact that He will hold every nation accountable for its actions. Another precious truth which can be gleaned from such a study is the place of prophecy as a confirmation of God's Word. The fact that these nations of ancient times met their individual destinies as prophesied in the Bible shows that this Bible is in very truth the Word of God.

It is fitting that the burden of Babylon should stand first in Isaiah's list. Babylon was the rallying point of rebellion against God in the time just after the flood (Gen. 11). It was apparently the place where idolatry originated and is a suitable representation throughout the Old Testament of the idolatrous, pagan world-system in opposition to God. (This symbolism is carried over

into the New Testament in the Book of Revelation.)
Furthermore Isaiah's prophecy is concerned to a very
large extent with the coming Babylonian captivity of
Judah, and it is therefore most appropriate that God's
people know ahead of time that their great enemy will
ultimately meet its doom. We are to see much more concerning the destruction of Babylon and of its idols in the
second part of Isaiah.

In the midst of God's pronouncement of judgment
upon Babylon there is mention of mercy for His people
(14:1).

The burden of Babylon also contains a mysterious
passage concerning a being called "Lucifer" (14:12).
One must admit that this is an inference, but the prophecy certainly seems to go far beyond any earthly ruler, no
matter how powerful. It has been traditionally accepted as referring to Satan, the "prince of this world"
(John 12:31; 14:30; 16:11) and the "god of this age"
(II Cor. 4:4). The word which is translated in the Authorized Version by *Lucifer* ("light-bearer") is literally
a word which means "daystar." This is the false daystar,
in contrast to the Lord Jesus Christ, who is the true daystar (II Peter 1:19).

This passage should be compared with Ezekiel 28:12-
19, which seems to be a similarly cryptic reference to
Satan. Ezekiel views the career of Satan from the beginning forward to its end. Isaiah sees his career from its
end backward to its beginning. Many Bible students
consider Isaiah 14:12-17 to be the central passage in the
Bible on the origin of sin. The fall from Heaven which
is mentioned in Isaiah 14:12 is a prophecy. The sin or
moral fall described in the passage belongs to the date-
less past, but the final casting of Satan out of Heaven

apparently will not take place until the end-time, at the middle of the period often spoken of as the "seventieth week" of Daniel (Dan. 9; Rev. 12:9). We must be careful to hold to the teaching of the Bible and to avoid prevalent misconceptions which have been popularized by Milton's *Paradise Lost* and other literary works.

Some of the burdens given in this section found at least a partial fulfillment in the Assyrian invasions of the period, but there can be no question that there are also long vistas of prophecy intermingled with the immediate scene, for the next section clearly mentions "that day," which is, as has been said, a reference to Messianic times.

CHAPTER 7

THROUGH JUDGMENTS TO THE KINGDOM

ISAIAH'S REPETITION of themes has been mentioned previously. In chapters 24 through 27 we see again the sequence which we are continuing to encounter in this wonderful book. It is as though God would convince His people by sheer force of repetition. This, indeed, is the order of life and is not confined to Isaiah: first suffering, then glory. So it was with our Lord Jesus Christ:

> . . . When it [the Spirit] testified beforehand of the sufferings of Christ, and the glory that should follow (I Peter 1:11).

So it is with believers:

> . . . If so be that we suffer with him, that we may be also glorified together (Rom. 8:17).
> But the God of all grace, who hath called us unto his eternal glory by Christ Jesus, after that ye have suffered a while, make you perfect, establish, strengthen, settle you (I Peter 5:10).

So it will be with the nation of Israel.

The section may be fitted into the main outline in this way:

Part One: The Judgment of God (1–39)
    I. Opening Prophecies (1–6)

Troubles Followed by the Reign of the Lord of Hosts

Clearly at the beginning of chapter 24 the prophecy turns away from the burdens of the Gentile nations to God's own people. Judgments are coming, troubles such as will empty the land (v. 3). These judgments are retributive, for the sins of the people (v. 5). They will include the capture and desolation of the city of Jerusalem (v. 12). Even in the midst of terrible afflictions, however, there will be those who will glorify the LORD "in the fires" (v. 15). Always there is the remnant.

That this prophecy looks forward to the Babylonian captivity seems evident; yet that captivity manifestly does not exhaust the import of it, because the prophet looks ahead to "that day" (v. 21). The close of the chapter proves this, with its mention of the reign of Jehovah of hosts in Mount Zion (v. 23).

Praise to God for His Wonderful Works

The contemplation of God's works brings forth the exclamation of praise:

> O LORD, thou art my God; I will exalt thee, I will
> praise thy name; for thou hast done wonderful things; thy
> counsels of old are faithfulness and truth (v. 1).

In this chapter is an example of Old Testament teachings which are taken over and amplified in the New Testament. Verse 8 is certainly referred to by Paul in I Corinthians 15:54, and the second clause is restated in Revelation 7:17 and 21:4.

In that day God's people will be glad that they "have waited for him." What a contrast to the impatience of this restless world! Patient waiting is the seemingly difficult but sublime appointment of the people of God now. It will not always be so. The day of waiting, interminable though it sometimes seems, will have an end; the day of rejoicing in God's completed salvation will be eternal.

A Song of Salvation

Here is a song which cannot be sung in fullness of meaning just now. It will be sung "in that day" (v. 1). Happily, though, application can be made now. The believer in any period of history can find in God the perfect peace described in the song (v. 3). How many songs and hymns have been based upon this passage!

> Stayed upon Jehovah hearts are fully blessed,
> Finding as He promised, perfect peace and rest.

Best known of all, Toplady's immortal "Rock of Ages," the title taken from the literal Hebrew of verse 4:

> For in JAH JEHOVAH is the Rock of ages.

God's Indignation and the Regathering of Israel

The indignation refers to the Day of Jehovah, mentioned so many times elsewhere in the prophets. From this tribulation the remnant of Israel will be protected (v. 20; cf. Rev. 12). Then will ensue such a regathering of Israel as has not previously been known. This is undoubtedly the regathering mentioned by the Lord Jesus Christ in Matthew 24:31:

> And he shall send his angels with a great sound of a trumpet, and they shall gather together his elect from the four winds, from one end of heaven to the other.

CHAPTER 8

THE WOES

THERE ARE SEVERAL outstanding passages in the Word of God where repeated woes are pronounced emphatically and solemnly. One such is the castigation of the Pharisees by the Lord Jesus Christ, with its sevenfold "Woe to you, scribes and Pharisees, hypocrites" (Matt. 23). Another is the passage on the three terrible woes in the end-time, at the blowing of the last three trumpets (Rev. 8:13). Another is the series in the passage now being considered.

In order to keep in mind the over-all picture of the book, it is helpful to review the basic outline repeatedly. The present section has this connection:

Part One: The Judgment of God (1—39)

    I. Opening Prophecies (1—6)

    II. The Book of Immanuel (7—12)

    III. Burdens Upon the Nations (13—23)

    IV. Through Judgments to the Kingdom (24—27)

    V. Pronouncement of Woes (28—33)

        A. Woe to Ephraim (28:1-13)

        B. Warning to the Rulers of Judah (28:14-29)

        C. Woe to Ariel (29:1-24)

        D. Woe to the Egyptian Alliance (30:1—31:9)

        E. The Righteous King Who Shall Deliver (32:1—33:24)

Woe to Ephraim

The Northern Kingdom, Israel, is addressed as Ephraim because of the prominent place which had always been assumed in it by the tribe of Ephraim. The reference to the "drunkards of Ephraim" (v. 1) is similar to the charges made against Israel in Amos 6 and Hosea 4. Those two prophets ministered directly to the Northern Kingdom, Amos just before and Hosea during Isaiah's time.

The woe upon Ephraim was not long in coming. Even as the prophet spoke Ephraim's flower was fading (v. 1). Assyria was about to tread the kingdom underfoot.

The Word of God frequently stresses the evil of drunkenness. It views it not as a weakness to be pitied, but as a sin to be condemned. While we can and should be compassionate toward the drunkard, we must not allow our sympathy to become maudlin, nor must we lose the clear perspective of Scripture.

Perhaps the most terrible thing about the drunkenness mentioned in this passage is that it touched those who were in places of leadership and responsibility (v. 7).

Warning to the Rulers of Judah

Nothing is more detestable than sneering unbelief in God. The leaders of Judah, who should have learned from the awful example of Israel, smugly relied upon their unholy treaties of alliance, unmindful of the promises and warnings of God.

In contrast to their refuge of lies (v. 15) God affirms that He will set up a sure foundation (v. 16). Who can deny that here again is a glimpse of the Messiah, who is spoken of in other parts of Scripture as the "cornerstone"?

This is the glory of Isaiah, that he constantly turns our thoughts toward Him who is our Immanuel, our Prince of peace, our Rock of Ages, our chief Cornerstone. Some will protest that it is fanciful and arbitrary to find a reference to Christ in this place. Not so; the Holy Spirit knows what He is about. We are not dealing with human theories about human writings, but with the realities of the Word of God. In I Peter 2:6 this verse is quoted as referring to Christ. Which shall it be, unbelieving rationalism or unwavering acceptance of the divine origin and unity of the Holy Scriptures?

Woe to Ariel

Jerusalem is now addressed (29:1) under the poetic name of Ariel ("the lion of God"). Here again there seems to be a blending of events near at hand with those in the far distant future. Near at hand was the invasion of the Assyrians under Sennacherib. Far away was the invasion of the land of Israel in the end-time shortly before the establishment of the Messianic kingdom. The judgment is because of hypocrisy on the part of those who were ostensibly the people of God. They were addicted to a formalistic religion which did not touch the heart (v. 13). As always in the prophecy, the judgment is not total. There is a glimpse of future restoration and glory (vv. 17-24).

Woe to the Egyptian Alliance

One of the hardest lessons which the people of God have to learn is that of total dependence upon God. It was the natural tendency when the powerful Assyrian

Empire threatened little Judah to turn to the only world-power that seemed capable of standing up to Assyria. That was Egypt.

God chides His people with a lack of trust in Himself. Egypt, He warns, cannot help. The people of Judah are "rebellious children" (v. 1), a title reminiscent of chapter 1. How often such a scene has been repeated in the history of God's people. The conflict between reason and faith is often a bitter one, chiefly because the reason is the reason of expediency. It is not actually reasonable because it leaves out the one all-important factor, the Person of God. The old saying, "One with God is a majority," remains true, but how often unheeded. The false prophets who advised an Egyptian alliance were listened to because they advocated action in a terrible emergency. The impatience of the human heart was not satisfied by the admonition of the true prophet of God:

> For thus saith the Lord GOD, the Holy One of Israel;
> In returning and rest shall ye be saved; in quietness and
> in confidence shall be your strength: and ye would not
> (v. 15).

This is not a mere quietism or passivism that is enjoined. It is a returning to *God;* it is a rest in *God.* Not a reliance upon quietness, but a reliance upon Him who alone can give quietness to the restless soul of man. This is in contrast to a peculiar philosophy of the world which is often heard—"Just have faith and everything will be all right." Faith in what? Or—more to the point—in whom? God is the answer to all problems.

"And ye would not." Centuries later the Lord Jesus Christ in His lament over Jerusalem, uttered these same words (Matt. 23:37). Men are ever prone to blame God for their troubles, when they themselves are the cause.

"Ye would not." Rebellion against God, unthinkable abomination, yet how often undertaken! Unreasoning madness!

But man's rebellion, no matter how reprehensible, cannot forever keep God from manifesting His grace. God promises to these people, undeserving as they are, deliverance from the Assyrian (v. 31). And when the deliverance comes, it will come in such a way that all can see that God did it.

The Righteous King Who Shall Deliver

Here is the answer to the world's unrest: "A king shall reign in righteousness" (32:1). Kings have reigned with varying degrees of ability and success, but there has never been any king like this. No doubt Hezekiah was relatively righteous as compared with his father, Ahaz. Nevertheless in this passage we look again to Messianic times; we see the One who is always either in view or just out of view in this book, our Lord Jesus Christ Himself. He is perfectly righteous, and He can reign in righteousness. Many who would like to have world-peace will not want it to come in this way. "The effect of righteousness will be peace." When a king reigns in righteousness, unrighteous people may well tremble in fear.

A distinction is made between the nation as a whole and the godly remnant. It is the remnant which speaks in 33:2:

> O LORD, be gracious unto us; we have waited for thee;
> be thou their arm every morning, our salvation also in the
> time of trouble.

While the Book of Isaiah is filled with figures of speech

and poetic language in general, one must not suppose
that these figures and this language represent a visionary world of unreality. They point to a real situation.
Some day such words as these will be literally true:

> The LORD is exalted; for he dwelleth on high: he hath
> filled Zion with judgment and righteousness (v. 5).

Over and over again the sequence is repeated—judgment then comfort, judgment then comfort. Isaiah is
like a glorious symphony in which these two contrasting
themes are woven together in new and interesting har-
monies, so that there is continual repetition without
monotony.

CHAPTER 9

JEHOVAH'S INDIGNATION AND THE BLOSSOMING DESERT

AFTER THE SECTION on the woes, the prophet calls upon all nations to hear another summation of God's purposes.

> Come near, ye nations, to hear; and hearken, ye people: let the earth hear, and all that is therein; the world, and all things that come forth of it. For the indignation of the LORD is upon all nations, and his fury upon all their armies: he hath utterly destroyed them, he hath delivered them to the slaughter (34:1, 2).

One hesitates to press this point so much, yet it is pressed in the book itself. First the indignation, then the blessing. The order is never varied.

Jehovah's Indignation

Some people refuse to believe that God manifests anger. The Scriptures, however, frequently speak of the wrath of God, and show that there will be a time when His righteousness will be vindicated. His indignation is not the vengeful, selfish anger of sinful human beings, but rather the holy wrath of outraged majesty. God would not be God if He allowed evil to go on forever unpunished and unchecked. As the prophet says, this indignation of Jehovah is directed against nations universally. This undoubtedly looks forward to the time when the Lord Jesus Christ will return to take over the government of the earth.

This "day of the LORD'S vengeance" (v. 8) is graphically described in other passages of Scripture, both in the Old Testament and the New, notably in the Book of Revelation. The truly believing heart can rest in the knowledge that things are going to be different in God's good time—wrongs are to be righted, evil recompensed, and good rewarded. It was important for the people of Israel to know this as they faced the immediate future, bleak with the thought of judgment for the nation's sins. As they beheld the terrible iniquity of the pagan nations round about, some of which were to be the instruments of Israel's judgment, they need not question God or rail at Him in unbelief. Those nations too would receive the due reward of their deeds.

In the face of a passage such as this it is strange indeed that some people can speak of the provincialism of the Old Testament, as if the people of Israel thought of Jehovah as only a tribal or national God who had no concern for other peoples and nations. One of the dominant notes in Isaiah is *universality*. All nations are constantly in view. The salvation which is offered is universal, and the judgment which is to come is universal—"the indignation of the LORD is upon *all* nations."

The Blossoming Desert

Chapter 35 is a wonderful and poetic description of blessings which will accompany the reign of the Messiah. The miracles of healing which the Lord Jesus Christ

performed during His earthly ministry were credentials
of His Messiahship and were a foreshadowing of marvelous conditions during the Millennium.

Here nature is pictured as reflecting the glories which
are to come upon God's people. We are told in the New
Testament that the "whole creation groaneth and travail-
eth in pain together until now" (Rom. 8:22). This
chapter is a prophecy of the time when the groaning will
be over, when the material earth will be "delivered from
the bondage of corruption into the glorious liberty of
the children of God" (Rom. 8:21).

This chapter furnishes another illustration of Isaiah's
use of constantly recurring themes. Here the highway
is mentioned prominently again:

> And an highway shall be there, and a way, and it shall
> be called The way of holiness; the unclean shall not pass
> over it; but it shall be for those: the wayfaring men,
> though fools, shall not err therein (v. 8).

This thought of the highway, incidentally, is one of the
many evidences for the unity of the Book of Isaiah (cf.
11:16; 40:3).

At the end of the chapter the "ransomed of the
LORD" are seen returning to Zion with unspeakable
joy. This same idea is repeated in 51:11. How wonderful to know that the One who furnished Israel's ransom
is our Redeemer also!

> For even the Son of man came not to be ministered
> unto, but to minister, and to give his life a ransom for
> many (Mark 10:45).

> For there is one God, and one mediator between God
> and men, the man Christ Jesus; who gave himself a ran-
> som for all, to be testified in due time (I Tim. 2:5, 6).

CHAPTER 10

HISTORICAL INTERLUDE

CHAPTERS 36 through 39 of Isaiah should be compared with II Kings 18-20 and II Chronicles 29-32. II Kings 19 and Isaiah 37 are identical.

These chapters, besides showing some of the historical background of Isaiah's prophecies, also bridge the gap, so to speak, between the Assyrian period and the Babylonian period. In Isaiah's day the chief enemy was Assyria, and that is reflected in the prophecies given during the time of Ahaz as well as in the actual invasion of Judah by Sennacherib which is described in this section. But Isaiah's message had most to do with the coming *Babylonian* captivity. These historical chapters show how Babylon first came to have contact with Judah, and foreshadow that coming danger.

God's Deliverance from Sennacherib

The first verse of chapter 36 contains one of the few dates mentioned in the book. By this time Assyria had swallowed up the Northern Kingdom of Israel and of course considered the litle kingdom of Judah an easy prey. When we realize that the city of Jerusalem was only about ten miles from the border between Israel and Judah, we can see how simple it was for the Assyrian ruler to deploy his forces against it. Imagine the alarm in the city as word came of the fall of one town after another to the Assyrian invaders.

Now comes a delegation from the Assyrian king, led by the scornful Rabshakeh. Only one thing spoken by the Assyrian was true—that Egypt could not be depended upon for safety (v. 6). Berating the emissaries of Judah and actually claiming the support of Jehovah, the Assyrian general hurls an insulting message to the people of Jerusalem on the wall.

That which doomed the purpose of the Assyrians to failure was their blasphemous comparison of God with the gods of conquered nations (vv. 18-20).

Hezekiah was a man of prayer. He sent immediately for the prophet Isaiah. Isaiah, far from being troubled, simply sent a message back to the godly king:

> Thus saith the LORD, Be not afraid of the words that thou hast heard, wherewith the servants of the king of Assyria have blasphemed me. Behold, I will send a blast upon him, and he shall hear a rumor, and return to his own land; and I will cause him to fall by the sword in his own land (37:6, 7).

Rabshakeh's return to his master was the occasion for another threatening, blasphemous message, this time in the form of a letter to King Hezekiah. The king knew what to do in such a situation. He "spread it before the LORD" (v. 14). The prayer of Hezekiah is an eloquent answer to those who allege that the Old Testament teaches a polytheistic or henotheistic religion. It is sometimes said by destructive critics of the Bible that the Hebrews in Old Testament times thought of Jehovah as one among many gods, although He was their particular God. Such a theory is a travesty upon the Old Testament. Hezekiah knew that the so-called gods of the nations were nonentities, and proclaimed it as clearly as the apostle Paul does in the New Testament (cf. v. 19 with I Cor. 8:4-6).

No doubt many in Hezekiah's time doubted or wondered at the prophecy which God gave through Isaiah in answer to the king's prayer. Certainly from a human point of view the Assyrian army seemed more than capable of conquering the city of Jerusalem. But Sennacherib and Rabshakeh did not know God; they had left Him out of account in their calculations, as unsaved men always do. It was He who defended the city (v. 35). The thirty-seventh chapter closes with a very brief statement of the widespread destruction brought about in the Assyrian army by the Angel of Jehovah (v. 36) and with the subsequent murder of Sennacherib in Nineveh by two of his own sons (v. 38). Secular historians have to admit that the Assyrian army withdrew because of some catastrophe. It is rather pathetic, but in a way somewhat laughable, to read their lame "explanations." One well-known historian blames the withdrawal on a pestilence brought on by the unhealthful marshes in which the army was encamped. That was quite a pestilence, which killed 185,000 men in one night!

Hezekiah's Illness and Its Aftermath

This historical interlude in Isaiah is really concerned with two main events in the reign of Hezekiah. The first, as we have seen, was the Assyrian invasion and withdrawal. The second is the king's serious illness and his recovery in answer to prayer. Isaiah 38 contains a very beautiful psalm written by King Hezekiah after his miraculous recovery (vv. 9-20). It is a striking testimony

of the faith of this remarkable man. Hezekiah recognized
that salvation was even more important than the recovery of his physical health:

> Behold, for peace I had great bitterness: but thou hast in
> love to my soul delivered it from the pit of corruption:
> for thou hast cast all my sins behind thy back (v. 17).

Yet even godly men can make serious mistakes. Hezekiah, for all his faith and prayerfulness, seems to have
given way to pride. In another passage God tells us that
the incident of the Babylonian envoys was permitted by
God as a test of Hezekiah (II Chron. 32:31). In this
test he did not come out so admirably. Each of us can
learn the lesson of our need of constant trust and dependence upon God. Victory in one battle does not
automatically insure victory in the next. "Wherefore
let him that thinketh he standeth take heed lest he fall"
(I Cor. 10:12).

This event shows the historical background of the
later Babylonian captivity, which is such an important
theme in Isaiah's prophecy, especially in the second part
of the book which now begins.

CHAPTER 11

THE COMFORT OF GOD

MENTION HAS ALREADY BEEN MADE in chapter 2 of the general theme and the arrangement of the second part of Isaiah. This part of the book looks through and beyond the Babylonian captivity, which was announced by Isaiah to King Hezekiah at the close of chapter 39. The general theme is expressed in the opening verse of chapter 40:

> Comfort ye, comfort ye my people, saith your God.

The prophet in this section is allowed to assume an ideal point of view and to see the captivity as already past, although it did not begin until long after his own time. As mentioned previously, this part of the book is divided into three sections of nine chapters each, the sections being marked off by the refrain of "no peace . . . to the wicked" (48:22; 57:21).

Recapitulating the basic outline as we have noticed it earlier we see:

Part One: The Judgment of God (1–39)

Part Two: The Comfort of God (40–66)

    I. Deliverance of God's People (40–48)

    II. The Suffering Servant as the Redeemer (49–57)

    III. The Glorious Consummation (58–66)

Each of these sections seems to be arranged symmetrically. In this part of Isaiah the present chapter divisions apparently followed rather closely the logical divisions of the prophet's message. In the first nine chapters (40—48) the thought centers about the deliverance from Babylon which is to be brought about by Cyrus, the Persian king. Cyrus is mentioned by name in the very heart of the section (44:28; 45:1). Throughout the section a contrast is drawn between Israel and the nations and between Jehovah and the false gods. Above and beyond the deliverance of the nation from Babylon is the recognition of a greater deliverance through the Messiah, the Lord Jesus Christ.

The Comfort of God for Delivered Israel

The opening of chapter 40 strikes the keynote for all that follows in this part of the book. What God purposes for His people He calls upon men also to do: "Comfort ye . . . my people."

These opening verses look toward a time when judgment will have ended, when Jerusalem will have paid enough for her iniquity. The basis of the comfort is given in the next paragraph (vv. 3-5). The comfort is possible because of the coming Messiah, whose herald is now introduced:

> The voice of him that crieth in the wilderness, Prepare ye the way of the LORD . . . (v. 3).

The New Testament shows that this is a prophetic reference to John the Baptist, the forerunner of Christ (Matt. 3:3; Mark 1:3; Luke 3:4-6; John 1:23).

As always in the Old Testament prophets the two comings of Christ are not distinguished, but are blended

together. The prophecies of verses 4 and 5 were not
completely fulfilled at His first advent, although partially so. When He comes again, there will be complete fulfillment (cf. Rev. 1:7 with John 1:14; II Peter 1:16-18;
and I John 1:1, 2).

The guaranty of the comfort which is promised is the
Word of God in its everlastingness (vv. 6-8). These
verses are alluded to in I Peter 1:24, 25. The Gospel
brings out the frailty in men, but God's Word is sure.

The comfort is proclaimed in the announcement of
the same One who was called earlier in Isaiah Immanuel
(7:14). Here the awe-inspiring statement is made: "Be-
hold your God!" In these beautiful verses we see both the
strength and the tenderness of the Saviour. His characterization as a shepherd is in harmony with the use of that
title for God in a number of Old Testament passages, and
foreshadows the application of the title by the Lord Jesus
to Himself in John 10:11 (cf. also Heb. 13:20, 21; I Peter
5:4).

The fortieth chapter contains next a description of the
character and omnipotence of God (vv. 12-31). The
paragraph abounds in rhetorical questions (cf. Job 38)
which awaken one to a sense of God's almighty power.
In verse 28 God is seen as eternal, omnipotent, and of
infinite wisdom. The chapter closes with the encourag-
ing truth that because God is all-powerful He can give
strength to those who need it.

Further Proof of the Power and Deity of God

In this chapter (41) God hurls a challenge at the idolatrous nations. There is a contrast between the first
verse, and the last verse of the preceding chapter. Those

who wait upon Jehovah will renew their strength, but how are the idolaters to do so?

One must keep in mind constantly that the prophecy has to do primarily with the deliverance of Israel from Babylon. The human deliverer has not yet been named, but he comes into view in verse 2: "the righteous man from the east." The power of Cyrus, the Persian king, is said to come from God's overruling purpose.

God next addresses the nation of Israel (v. 8), calling the nation "my servant." This expression is noteworthy, for it is used in different senses in the later chapters, and many students of Scripture—especially among the Jewish people—have failed to recognize these differences. Sometimes in Isaiah the term *servant* is used for the entire nation of Israel, as here; sometimes it is used for the godly portion of the people, the remnant (e.g., 43:10); and, most important of all, sometimes for the Messiah.

There is indication in this passage, as in so many other parts of Scripture, that God overrules in human history. He is the Sovereign; His "kingdom ruleth over all" (Ps. 103:19).

In the latter part of the chapter the challenge which was implied at the beginning is brought out in detail. It is a call to the idols to prophesy:

> Show the things that are to come hereafter, that we may know that ye are gods . . . (v. 23).

Prediction of the future is the prerogative of God alone, because He alone is the all-knowing One. This fact is often asserted in Isaiah. As has been said, prophecy is the seal which God has put on His Word to show its genuineness. It authenticates the Scripture.

CHAPTER 12

MESSIAH, THE SERVANT, AND
ISRAEL, THE SERVANT

The Servant Who Will Bring Judgment

CHAPTER 42 is clearly a Messianic passage. Much the same thought is developed later in chapters 49 and 53 concerning the Servant. In the first nine verses of the chapter we see the Lord Jesus Christ in His relationship to the Gentiles.

This characterization of Christ as the Servant of Jehovah, first brought out in this evangelical prophet, is expanded in the Gospels, especially in Mark, which thus shows a close connection with Isaiah, and is recognized by the church in the Book of Acts.

This very passage is quoted in Matthew 12:17-21, where the ministry of the Lord Jesus Christ is said to be a fulfillment of the prophecy. It should be noticed again, however, that the two advents of Christ are as usual mingled together. There is the ministry of Christ in weakness and the ministry of Christ in power; the despised and rejected Christ, and the conquering and judging Christ.

In contrast to the destructive critical view which sees the ancient Israelites as being entirely selfish in their concept of God, we see the reality here—a recognition that the salvation of the Messiah will extend to the Gentiles. This is not the first time that this truth has been enunciated in Isaiah (cf. ch. 9), nor is it the last.

The challenge to idols is carried on throughout this section. Babylon, the center and hotbed of idolatry, is to be destroyed. God is going to see to it that idols do not get the glory that rightfully belongs only to Him:

> I am the LORD: that is my name: and my glory will I not give to another, neither my praise to graven images (v. 8).

With the call to sing a new song (v. 10) comes a declaration of the power of God which is manifested through His servant, the Messiah. This song is comparable to the exquisite song of salvation in chapter 12.

The chapter closes with a rebuke of Israel for unfaithfulness (vv. 18-25).

Israel's Privilege and Responsibility as the Servant

The nation of Israel is now addressed. God reminds the people of Israel that He has chosen them (vv. 1-10). This is a constantly reiterated marvel in Scripture of God's grace. God bears a special relationship to this nation, not only as Creator, but as Saviour and Redeemer. The title, "Holy One of Israel," used in both parts of the Book of Isaiah, shows that special relationship.

God next reminds His people of His intervention for them in the past (vv. 11-17). Just as God delivered through the Red Sea in the time of Moses (v. 16), so He will deliver now. In fact, the new deliverance of God will so overshadow the old that the "former things" need not be remembered (vv. 18-20).

The grace of God stands out in all its brilliance when

compared with the ungratefulness of Israel. God formed Israel for Himself (v. 21) and longed for fellowship, but Israel did not call upon Him (v. 22), and in turn Israel wearied God with its iniquities (v. 24). The judgment must come because of the nation's sins; nevertheless God is the One who forgives sin:

> I, even I, am he that blotteth out thy transgressions for mine own sake, and will not remember thy sins (v. 25).

CHAPTER 13

CYRUS AS GOD'S ANOINTED

WE HAVE COME NOW almost to the center of this first
section in the second part of Isaiah. Remember
that the second part of the book is in three sections of
nine chapters each and that there is a symmetrical arrangement, with the central thought of each section coming into prominence in the middle of the section. This
section may be outlined thus:

I. Deliverance for Israel (40—48)

   A. The Comfort of God (40)

    B. Further Proof of Jehovah's Power and Deity
     (41)

      C. Jehovah's Servant Who Will Bring Judg-
       ment (42)

       D. Israel's Privilege and Responsibility as the
        Servant (43)

        E. The Powerful God and the Powerless Idols
         (44)

       F. God's Purposes Through Cyrus, His
        Anointed (45)

      G. Judgment upon Babylon's Idols (46)

     H. Judgment upon the Babylonian Empire (47)

    I. Exhortations to the Impenitent and Unbeliev-
     ing (48)

The Powerful God and the Powerless Idols

This chapter (44) opens with promises to Israel (vv. 1-5). These promises are not based upon what Israel has done or will do, but on what God has done, upon God's own love and grace. Twice He speaks of Israel as His "chosen," using the second time the symbolic name, *Jesurun* ("Upright"), which He used in Deuteronomy 32:15 and 33:5, 26. This is the genius of the Word of God, that one part alludes to other parts, so that the person who is making a continual study of Scripture is always being amazed and delighted at the new connections, at the new parallels, at the new glimpses of truth placed there by the infinitely wise Author.

Again God makes mention of His omniscience as the proof that He can fulfill His promises (vv. 6-8). It is perhaps hard for many of us today to see the point of some of these allusions. We need to realize that the people of Israel lived in an almost completely idolatrous environment, that Israel was a little island of monotheism in a great sea of polytheism. Worse than that, it was not even what God intended it to be, for a great many of the people of Israel in Isaiah's day were idolaters. Even Hezekiah's reforms did not permanently affect the mass of the kingdom of Judah. Consequently most of the people knew from first-hand experience what an idol was. The tragic reality was that many of those who by position ought to have been the people of God were making and falling down before idols.

Hence the relevancy of the magnificent satire in this chapter (vv. 9-20). It is always a source of astonishment that men would attribute supernatural power to something which they had fashioned with their own hands.

Isaiah paints a picture that is unexcelled for its simple
irony, of a man who uses part of a log to warm himself
and to cook his food, and then makes another part of the
same piece of wood into a "god" (vv. 15-17)! Of course
practically all idolaters, ancient and modern, have
claimed that they do not worship the image, but only
that which is represented by the image. In reality most
of them, whether they acknowledge it or not, are worshiping the image; and even if they are not, they are not
worshiping the one true and living God, who is Spirit,
and who cannot be represented by any image.

> And none considereth in his heart, neither is there knowl-
> edge or understanding to say, I have burned part of it in
> the fire; yea, also I have baked bread upon the coals there-
> of; I have roasted flesh, and eaten it: and shall I make the
> residue thereof an abomination? shall I fall down to the
> stock of a tree? He feedeth on ashes: a deceived heart
> hath turned him aside, that he cannot deliver his soul, nor
> say, Is there not a lie in my right hand? (vv. 19, 20).

Yet again we hear the glorious strains of a song of redemption for Israel. This is a song unconfined, a song
of Heaven and earth. God says to Jerusalem, which certainly was inhabited in Isaiah's time, but which was to
become uninhabited and desolate in the Babylonian captivity, "Thou shalt be inhabited" (v. 26). Now He mentions the man who is to be the instrument of this deliverance:

> That saith of Cyrus, He is my shepherd, and shall per-
> form all my pleasure; even saying to Jerusalem, Thou shalt
> be built: and to the temple, Thy foundation shall be laid
> (v. 28).

This is actually the crux of the problem as far as the
attitude of critics toward the Book of Isaiah is concerned.
This has already been noted earlier. Here is Isaiah in the

eighth century B.C. announcing Cyrus as the restorer of
the people to Jerusalem, Cyrus who lived in the sixth
century B.C. This is not the only place, however, where
God has named a man long before his birth. There was
such a prophecy of Josiah almost three centuries before
he was born (I Kings 13:2).

The whole point of the passage is that God, the omnis-
cient God, is the One who announces events beforehand.
That is the proof of His deity. The destructive critics
who say that this passage must have been written in the
sixth century by some otherwise unknown prophet in
Babylon ("Deutero-Isaiah") are making the same stupid
mistake that the idolaters of Isaiah's day were making.
They are like the Sadducees of another time, to whom the
Lord Jesus Christ said, "Ye do err, not knowing the scriptures, nor the power of God" (Matt. 22:29).

The historical fulfillment of this prophecy is told in
II Chronicles 36:22, 23, and Ezra 1:1-11. Cyrus gave the
decree for the rebuilding of the temple in Jerusalem in
536 B.C., almost two hundred years after this prophecy.

God's Purposes Through Cyrus, His Anointed

Chapter 45, of course, is very closely related to the
preceding chapter. At the end of chapter 44 Cyrus is in-
troduced in the third person. At the beginning of chap-
ter 45 he is addressed directly in the second person.
There is a prophetic statement of the victories of Cyrus
(vv. 1-8). Cyrus is the only Gentile king who is called
God's "anointed." Since this is the translation of the
Hebrew word which we spell in English as *Messiah*,
Cyrus is in a sense a type of the Anointed One, the Lord
Jesus Christ. Typology is often misunderstood and

abused. A type is a divinely appointed prophetic symbol, usually of Christ. When a person or a thing is
called a type, that does not alter its literal meaning or
deny its historical reality. Cyrus was a Persian king, and
we have no evidence that he ever really knew the true
God, although the Persian religion was relatively free
from the gross idolatries of the Babylonians. Consequently when it is asserted that Cyrus is a type of Christ, it is
not said that he was like the Lord Jesus Christ in every
respect. The only intended resemblance is in the fact
that Cyrus was the anointed one who delivered the people of Israel from their captivity. As such he points us to
the greater Anointed One who saves His people from
their sins.

Though Cyrus did not know God (v. 4), God used
him to work out His purposes for His people Israel.
It will come undoubtedly as a shock to some people to
discover that God in His sovereign providence regulates
the affairs of mighty nations like Babylon and the Medo-
Persian Empire for the welfare of the widely despised
and ridiculed people of Israel. Though Cyrus did not
know it, it was God who enabled him to destroy the power of the Babylonian Empire. The transition of power
from Babylon to the Medes and the Persians is seen in
the Bible in the Book of Daniel, written by Daniel who
lived in that time, that is, the time when the fictional
"Deutero-Isaiah" of the critics is supposed to have lived.
(Ludicrously enough, some of those same critics maintain
that Daniel could not have been written by Daniel, but
must have been written by some unknown romancer of
the second century B.C.)

After the recital of the victories of Cyrus, God again
reverts to the theme of His salvation of Israel (vv. 9-17).

> But Israel shall be saved in the LORD with an everlasting salvation. . . . (v. 17).

The word *everlasting* is a cue to the fact that God has more in store for His people than deliverance from Babylon, wonderful as that will be. Cyrus the "messiah" is only a temporary shadow; Jesus Christ the Messiah is the eternal reality.

Here again, however, the message is clearly expounded that salvation through the Messiah is not to be restricted to the nation of Israel. Isaiah uses the expression which some of us may sometimes use without awareness of its origin: "the ends of the earth."

> Look unto me, and be ye saved, all the ends of the earth:
> for I am God, and there is none else (v. 22).

The poor, deluded idolaters of the Gentiles will yet be visited with the salvation of Jehovah. Messiah will yet reign in universal righteousness and peace. God's oath that all will some day be in subjection to Him will be fulfilled:

> That unto me every knee shall bow, every tongue shall swear (v. 23).

The New Testament echoes of this statement are not hard to find. The verse is directly quoted in Romans 14:11, and is most certainly alluded to in the great passage on the Person of Christ in Philippians 2:

> That at the name of Jesus every knee should bow, of things in heaven, and things in earth, and things under the earth; and that every tongue should confess that Jesus Christ is Lord, to the glory of God the Father (Phil. 2:10, 11).

CHAPTER 14

THE JUDGMENT OF BABYLON

T HE JUDGMENT which God was to bring upon the Babylonian Empire was described in the first part of Isaiah as the first of the burdens (ch. 13). There Babylon was seen in connection with other nations in a general view of Gentile judgment. At this point the prophecy particularizes the judgment upon Babylon, viewing it, not only as something which is to happen to Babylon itself, but also as an object-lesson for Israel. It is only fitting that Babylon's downfall should be seen in connection with the deliverance of Israel, which is the general theme of this section.

The Doom of Babylon's Idols

Bel and Nebo, who are mentioned at the beginning of chapter 46, are two of the leading "gods" of Babylon. Here we view a graphic scene: Babylon's idols, unable to defend her, are themselves being carried into captivity. Laughable picture—for one who has the proper sense of humor! These are gods, bouncing and jolting along on the beasts of burden?

God says in effect to Israel, "These gods have to be carried, but I am the One who has carried you."

> Remember this, and show yourselves men: bring it again
> to mind, O ye transgressors. Remember the former things
> of old: for I am God, and there is none else; I am God,
> and there is none like me . . . (vv. 8, 9).

God tells these things ahead of time in order that when they do come to pass men may know His omniscience and His almighty power.

All of this constitutes a warning to transgressors to turn from their transgressions unto God.

Judgment upon the Babylonian Empire

Chapter 47 should be compared with what has already been said in chapters 13 and 14. This Babylonian Empire, sometimes called in history the Neo-Babylonian or Chaldean Empire, reached its height under Nebuchadnezzar, who captured and destroyed the city of Jerusalem in 586 B.C. This was naturally far in the future in Isaiah's time when this prophecy was written.

The Book of Daniel describes some of the conditions in the time of Nebuchadnezzar and afterward, and chapter 5 of that book records the historical fulfillment of the prophecy given here in Isaiah 47, when the city of Babylon was captured by the army of the Medes and the Persians.

Even in bringing judgment upon such a wicked nation as Babylon, God vindicates Himself. God has used Babylon as an instrument of His judgment upon His own people, Israel. Now Babylon is to be judged, not because of some arbitrary notion of God, but because Babylon is sinful:

> For thou hast trusted in thy wickedness: thou hast said,
> None seeth me. . . . (v. 10).

This principle is observed in other prophets. Jeremiah and Habakkuk particularly speak of it.

Babylon was teeming with all kinds of idols, with pagan priests, with astrologers, soothsayers, charlatans, and demon-inspired religionists. But none of them was able to help. They, along with the rest, were to be destroyed. No doubt, from a human point of view, there was much that was admirable in the achievements of the Babylonians. They had a relatively high state of civilization, grand buildings, a seemingly impregnable city; they were advanced in mathematics, astronomy, and literature. But the moral character of the Babylonian Empire was such that the people of God need not shed a tear over its downfall.

Exhortations to the Impenitent and Unbelieving

Instead of being concerned about the downfall of Babylon, Israel should be concerned about its own relationship to God. God had made known the things which were to come. Had His people profited from this revelation?

"Yea, thou heardest not; yea, thou knewest not" (v. 8).

This is something which many of God's people in New Testament times do not yet understand—the practical nature of prophecy. Many there are who study the details of prophecy simply because they find a fascination in the subject. They are intrigued by it as if it were merely a cleverly constructed puzzle to be solved. They have missed the point. Prophecy ought to have some effect upon the daily living of God's people.

> Thus saith the LORD, thy Redeemer, the Holy One of
> Israel; I am the LORD thy God which teacheth thee to
> profit, which leadeth thee by the way that thou shouldest
> go. O that thou hadst hearkened to my commandments!
> then had thy peace been as a river . . . (vv. 17, 18).

Seeing God's sovereign control of history ought to
solemnize us, so that we should give over our lives to
Him, so that we should recognize His complete right
to us.

This whole section of nine chapters has emphasized the
almighty power of God in contrast to the idols. It
closes with this powerful appeal to accept the salvation
of God, and with the solemn warning, "There is no peace,
saith the LORD, unto the wicked" (48:22).

CHAPTER 15

THE SUFFERING AND FUTURE GLORY OF THE SERVANT

W E HAVE NOW ARRIVED at the second section of part two of Isaiah. Since this part of the book is arranged according to a definite and identifiable plan, we can readily see that this is the center of the teaching on the comfort of God. In order to have this clearly before us, let us think again of the outline of the book.

ISAIAH—THE SALVATION OF JEHOVAH

Part One: The Judgment of God (1—39)
Part Two: The Comfort of God (40—66)

  I. Deliverance of God's People (40—48)
  II. The Suffering Servant as the Redeemer (49—57)

    A. God's Salvation through the Servant (49)
    B. Exhortations to the Unbelieving (50)
    C. Exhortations to the Righteous (51)
    D. Zion's Joy in the Lord's Deliverance (52:1-12)
    E. THE SUFFERING SERVANT OF JEHOVAH (52:13—53:12)
    F. Restoration of Israel to the Place of Blessing (54)

God's Salvation Through the Servant

While the idea of the Servant is constantly changing, sometimes referring to Israel and sometimes to the Messiah, as we have seen, this section emphasizes the Messianic aspect. Christ was introduced as the Servant in the previous section (ch. 42), but here His Person and work are more fully set forth.

As chapter 49 opens, it is the Servant who is speaking. The first half of the chapter tells of the exaltation of Christ (vv. 1-13); the second half, of the glory which is to come to Zion (14-26).

Taking up an idea which has been given before (45: 22), God says to the Servant:

I will also give thee for a light to the Gentiles, that thou mayest be my salvation unto the end of the earth (v. 6).

Through this marvelous salvation Zion is to be comforted. Zion is a title used often in the Scripture for the city of Jerusalem, being originally the hill upon which the ancient citadel was erected. In her captivity and judgment Zion is tempted to think that God has forgotten and forsaken her (v. 14), but God assures her that this cannot be (vv. 15, 16). In glorifying Israel God will make use of Gentiles, and will hold to a strict accounting all those who have oppressed His people (v. 26).

Exhortations to the Unbelieving

God goes on to show His people (ch. 50) that He has
not rejected them. No, God has not rejected them, but
their sufferings arise from their own sins (vv. 1-3). God
asks, "Wherefore, when I came, was there no man?"
(v. 2). God "came" by His servants the prophets (cf.
Heb. 1:1), and later by the Servant Himself, God's own
beloved Son (cf. Heb. 1:2; John 1:10, 11), but Israel
gave no proper response. Even Christ, when He came,
was rejected.

The next paragraph of the chapter (vv. 4-9) amplifies
the thought of the opposition to Jehovah's Servant:

> I gave my back to the smiters, and my cheeks to them
> that plucked off the hair: I hid not my face from shame
> and spitting (v. 6).

This is not Isaiah who is speaking, nor is it an ideal-
ized portrait of the nation of Israel. It is an individual,
not a group; it is *The Servant;* it is the Lord Jesus Christ.
This verse finds its historical fulfillment in the accounts
of the sufferings of Christ in the Gospels:

> Then did they spit in his face, and buffeted him . . .
> (Matt. 26:67).

> And they spit upon him, and took the reed, and smote
> him on the head (Matt. 27:30).

These and a number of other passages show the ap-
plicability of the prophecy in Isaiah to the Lord Jesus
Christ and to Him exclusively.

The chapter closes with a mention of two ways: the
way of trust (v. 10) and the way of sorrow (v. 11). Dependence upon God or dependence upon self—the one
leads to peace and salvation, the other to destruction.
These are in essence the same two ways presented in the

First Psalm and in the words of the Lord Jesus Christ in Matthew 7:13, 14.

Exhortations to Those Who Follow after Righteousness

It might be said that the previous exhortations were addressed to the nation as a whole, while these (ch. 51) are addressed to the godly remnant, those "that follow after righteousness" (v. 1). The first part of the chapter gives comforting assurances to those who seek the Lord (vv. 1-16); the remainder again speaks of the triumph of Jerusalem and the destruction of her enemies (vv. 17-23).

In the first part of Isaiah the hand of the Lord was seen as stretched out in judgment. Now the arm of the Lord is called upon to awake (v. 9). This is the arm of deliverance, mentioned again in 53:1. Again there is a reminder of God's mighty deliverance of His people at the time of the exodus from Egypt (vv. 9, 10). This is followed by the same joyous refrain which we have heard previously in 35:10:

> Therefore the redeemed of the LORD shall return, and come with singing unto Zion; and everlasting joy shall be upon their head: they shall obtain gladness and joy; and sorrow and mourning shall flee away (v. 11).

It is such characteristic repetitions of Isaiah, such interweaving of themes and refrains, such reappearances of leading ideas, that help to show the perfect unity of the book.

The same God who created the heavens and who divided the sea for Israel in her earlier history will bring about this glorious deliverance. Jerusalem, which has

drunk the cup of God's fury to the dregs, has the promise
that she will never drink of it again (v. 22). Instead, the
oppressors and afflicters of Israel shall drink of it (v. 23).

Zion's Joy in the Lord's Deliverance

Again (as in 51:17) Jerusalem is called upon to awake
(52:1). Here the city of Jerusalem is pictured as a beautiful woman who has been prostrate in the dust, but who
is now to get up and sit upon the throne which God has
prepared for her (v. 2). Then the herald is pictured as
coming upon the mountains to proclaim God's reign
(v. 7). Paul makes an application of this in reference to
the Gospel in Romans 10:15. It is as though we have
made a complete cycle from chapter 40, for we read again
that God has comforted His people (v. 9). With God
both before and behind, Israel cannot but be safe (v. 12).

CHAPTER 16

THE SERVANT AS THE LAMB

CHAPTER 53, one of the best-known chapters of the
Word of God, is the middle chapter of the second
section and therefore the middle chapter of the whole
second part of Isaiah. Its position is no accident. It
gives to us a wonderful prophetic picture of the sufferings and death of the Lord Jesus Christ. The general
theme of the second part of Isaiah, as you may remember,
is: THE COMFORT OF GOD. The theme of the second section is: The Suffering Servant as the Redeemer.
It is this chapter which reveals to us in greater measure
than any other portion of the book the suffering of the
Servant.

Evidence That the Chapter Refers to Christ

Many, including orthodox Jews, deny that this chapter refers to the Lord Jesus Christ, but the proofs of its
Messianic character are many and varied.

For one thing, the one described in the prophecy is
said to be the Servant of Jehovah (52:13; 53:11). We
have already seen that sometimes Israel is called Jehovah's servant; in this chapter, however, the servant cannot be Israel, for an individual is pictured. Those who
are speaking in the chapter are Israel. Consequently the

89

Servant must be the Messiah, since the Messiah is called
the Servant in other places in Isaiah (ch. 42, 49).

Comparison with other prophetic passages shows that
this is Messianic. From Genesis 3:15 God in His Word
traces the line of descent of the Redeemer and keeps
adding details concerning Him. Some passages which can
be compared with this are: Psalm 22 (the psalm of the
cross); Psalm 69; Daniel 9:26; Zechariah 9:9; 12:10; 13:
7. It may also be added that this chapter is the climax
to similar passages in the Book of Isaiah itself (42:4;
49:4; 50:6).

There is, of course, also the ancient and uniform tradition. The ancient Jews, before the coming of the Lord
Jesus, regarded the passage as Messianic, and the church
has always so regarded it, with the exception of modern
rationalistic interpreters.

Add to these lines of evidence the negative one that
no other satisfactory interpretation has ever been advanced. Those who deny the Messianic meaning cannot
agree on any other interpretation.

Certainly an unprejudiced person who reads this chapter and then reads the Gospel records must admit that
the prophecy and the history fit perfectly when applied
to the Lord Jesus Christ.

All of these proofs, weighty as they are, are less important than the conclusive one now to be mentioned. That
is, the New Testament expressly declares that this is a
prophecy of Jesus Christ. There are at least eighty references to Isaiah (direct and indirect) in the New Testament, and the great majority of these are references to
this one chapter. When Philip met the Ethiopian treasurer on the desert road and was asked, concerning this

very chapter: "Of whom speaketh the prophet this? Of himself, or of some other man?" Philip did not hesitate. There is no equivocation in the statement of Scripture:

> Then Philip opened his mouth, and began at the same scripture, and preached unto him Jesus (Acts 8:35).

This is by no means the only quotation of this chapter in the New Testament. There are at least six direct quotations:

52:15 is quoted in Romans 15:21.

53:1 is quoted in John 12:38 and in Romans 10:16.

53:4 is quoted in Matthew 8:17.

53:5, 6 is quoted in I Peter 2:22-25.

53:7, 8 is quoted in Acts 8:32, 33.

53:12 is quoted in Mark 15:28 and Luke 22:37.

In addition to these specific quotations there are many more brief allusions to the terms found in the chapter. Here are some comparisons which will repay study:

Romans 4:25 with verse 5.

I Peter 1:19 with verse 7.

Revelation 5:6 with verse 7.

Revelation 7:14 with verse 7.

John 1:29, 36 with verses 7 and 11.

I John 3:5 with verses 9 and 11.

I Corinthians 15:3, 4 with verses 8-11.

II Corinthians 5:21 with verses 8-11.

The nineteenth century German commentator, Franz Delitzsch, writing on this chapter, said: "All the references in the New Testament to the Lamb of God (with which the corresponding allusions to the Passover are interwoven) spring from this passage in the Book of Isaiah. . . The dumb type of the Passover now finds a tongue."

The Structure of the Chapter

This chapter has been called the "holy of holies" of
Isaiah. The early church writer, Polycarp, spoke of it
as the "golden passional of the Old Testament." It is the
great connecting link between Psalm 22 and Psalm 110,
the former being the psalm of the cross and the latter the
psalm of Christ's royal priesthood. It seems likely that
all five of the major Levitical offerings are referred to in
the chapter, for the Lord Jesus Christ is the fulfillment
of all of them.

The fifty-third chapter should begin at 52:13. The
passage is in five paragraphs, each containing three verses.
Keeping as closely as possible to the wording of the passage itself, we can outline it thus:

The Suffering Servant of Jehovah   (52:13—53:12)
    The Servant Exalted   (52:13-15)
    The Servant Despised   (53:1-3)
    The Servant Wounded   (53:4-6)
    The Servant Cut Off   (53:7-9)
    The Servant Satisfied   (53:10-12)

The Servant Exalted

The first paragraph or strophe really gives us a sum-
mary of the whole prophecy. At the beginning Jehovah
calls upon men to look upon His Servant:

> Behold, my servant shall deal prudently, he shall be ex-
> alted and extolled, and be very high.

This looks on beyond the suffering to the glorious exaltation described in Philippians 2:8-11. The suffering
must come first, however:

> As many were astonied at thee; his visage was so marred
> more than any man, and his form more than the sons of
> men (v. 14).

How can one read of the torture inflicted upon the
"holy, harmless, undefiled" Son of God and Son of man
without being moved? Such torture, as described in
Matthew 26:67, 68 and 27:27-30, was to bring actual disfigurement to that unique countenance, such disfigurement as to cause great amazement.

The suffering becomes marvelously the pathway to
glory. Amazement at His disfigurement is turned into
wonder at His grace:

> So shall he sprinkle many nations; the kings shall shut
> their mouths at him: for that which had not been told them
> shall they see; and that which they had not heard shall
> they consider.

The Servant Despised

The Jews are right in considering this as a prophecy
of Israel, but they have Israel cast in the wrong role.
This is a picture of the nation of Israel in its future
national Day of Atonement (cf. Zech. 12:10) when the
people will at last recognize and acknowledge the Lord
Jesus as the Messiah. This is the prophetic presentation
of their musings at that time. They cannot comprehend
the reality all at once. Who would have believed it,
they say, that this "tender plant," this "root out of a
dry ground," this undesired One, this despised and rejected One is really the Messiah after all! They are not
referring to a report that they have made, but to a report
which came to them. In this exclamatory question they
admit their former unbelief:

> Who hath believed our report? and to whom is the arm
> of the LORD revealed? (53:1).

The lowliness of the Lord Jesus is described. While
there is reason to believe from other passages of Scripture
that the winsome character of the Lord Jesus appealed
even to some of the most hopeless of men, yet this prophecy makes clear that which some Christians have not yet
fully comprehended, that the Lord Jesus Christ did not
appear in such a way as to attract the natural man.
While the power of His deity was evident on occasion,
there was no mere glamor about Him. He lived His
earthly life in humble circumstances, not in worldly
pomp. The natural mind is all too ready to construe
meekness as weakness and to waste its adulation on the
proud and self-seeking. "No beauty that we should desire him" is the contemptuous but almost universal ver-
dict, except of those whom the Father in His grace drew
toward His beloved Son (John 6:44).

> He is despised and rejected of men; a man of sorrows,
> and acquainted with grief: and we hid as it were our faces
> from him; he was despised, and we esteemed him not (v.
> 3).

It seems inconceivable to some that the Lord Jesus
should be so despised. Here and there were the com-
paratively few disciples, the godly women who ministered
to His needs, the Roman centurion, the Syro-Phoenician
woman. But the great mass were ready to cry out, "Crucify him, crucify him!" Many who followed Him and
thronged about Him in His ministry were only eager to
see some exciting miracle or to eat of the miraculously
provided loaves (John 6:26). It is so even today. Many
who prate at length of the "lowly Nazarene" as a great
teacher and good man speak only in hollow mockery.

When the issue is joined, when the truths of the Gospel are considered, when His deity and substitutionary atonement are in question, then these too despise and reject Him. Who can estimate the guilt of the self-righteous religious leader who sneers at the precious blood of Christ?

There is an important lesson in this for believers. Why should we seek the approval of a world which despises our Lord? Why should we desire acceptance by men who reject Him?

Some day the godly remnant of Israel will be sorry for this rejection; some day they will turn in real repentance to Him.

The Servant Wounded

During His ministry on earth, the Lord Jesus entered sympathetically into the griefs and afflictions of men. This is the meaning of the first part of verse 4, as clearly explained in Matthew 8:17. There is no warrant for supposing that healing is "in the atonement," as some erroneously teach from this verse. Christ healed every manner of sickness and disease among the people, but He died for our sins, not for our illnesses. The godly remnant of Israel in a future day continue their prophetic musings:

> . . . Yet we did esteem him stricken, smitten of God, and afflicted. But he was wounded for our transgressions, he was bruised for our iniquities: the chastisement of our peace was upon him; and with his stripes we are healed.

Here is substitution. Israel in Christ's own day thought that He deserved to die. He was accused of and condemned for blasphemy. He was considered smitten of

God deservedly. Nevertheless He died, not for Himself,
but for others, and this prophecy is the assurance that
Israel will some day realize this blessed truth. This is
the heart of this wonderfully symmetrical second part of
Isaiah. There is no higher truth than this—that the sinless Son of God died on the cross for sinful man. One
can fully understand why Isaiah is called the prophet of
the Gospel.

> All we like sheep have gone astray; we have turned
> everyone to his own way; and the LORD hath laid on him
> the iniquity of us all.

One day the Lord Jesus looked compassionately upon
the multitudes of Israel "as sheep having no shepherd"
(Matt. 9:36). "Everyone to his own way . . ." That is
what men want. They think that they are free, that they
are working out their own destiny; instead, they are lost.

God in His infinite grace provided salvation for us
wandering sheep. Christ died for our sins. The expression "laid on him" means literally "to cause to strike with
great force." Paul explains it in these words:

> Him who knew no sin he made to be sin on our behalf,
> that we might become the righteousness of God in him (II
> Cor. 5:21, A.S.V.).

Peter comments on this passage:

> Who his own self bare our sins in his own body on the
> tree, that we, being dead to sins, should live unto righteous-
> ness: by whose stripes ye were healed. For ye were as
> sheep going astray: but are now returned to the Shepherd
> and Bishop [overseer] of your souls (I Peter 2:24, 25).

The Servant Cut Off

The Lord Jesus was not an unwilling victim, com-

pelled to go to the cross. No, He was the voluntary sacrifice. All the path from glory to Calvary was illumi-
nated by His "Lo, I come . . . to do thy will, O God"
(Heb. 10:7). Here indeed, as Delitzsch so aptly said, the
Passover "finds a tongue." All through the centuries
since Moses' time the Passover lambs had been killed, all
pointing forward to Someone, yet giving only a silent
and cryptic witness. Now that Someone is revealed, and
the sequence is perfectly clear. From Isaiah 53:7 to John
1:29 is but a step:

> Behold the Lamb of God, which taketh away the sin of
> the world.

The prophecy proceeds to speak of the thoughtlessness
of His generation. "Cut off out of the land of the living."
Condemned by His own people, yet graciously bearing
their transgressions. Daniel was likewise to speak of the
cutting off of Messiah (Dan. 9:26). With what seemingly irrelevant details prophecy is sometimes concerned!
Yet that which appears to be irrelevant furnishes proof
of the genuineness of the prophecy. There could be no
accidental fulfillment of such a prediction as this. He
who was crucified between two malefactors was buried
in the tomb of a rich man, Joseph of Arimathaea (Matt.
27:57).

The Servant Satisfied

Men see the death of the Lord Jesus only as a tragedy.
They imagine a visionary martyr, perhaps ahead of His
time, suffering and dying for His ideals. This is a travesty. God's Word shows that that which is in one sense
tragedy is the source of the deepest joy. What Christ
suffered at the hands of men was tragic. They took Him

and with "wicked hands" crucified and killed Him, as
Peter declared (Acts 2:23). In and through the tragedy,
nevertheless, God was working out His sovereign purpose
of grace. Isaiah emphasizes that:

> Yet it pleased the LORD to bruise him; he hath put him
> to grief: when thou shalt make his soul an offering for sin,
> he shall see his seed, he shall prolong his days, and the
> pleasure of the LORD shall prosper in his hand.

The most mysterious thing about the death of Christ,
and the most glorious, is that He was God's sacrificial
Lamb. In some way which we cannot comprehend He
took our place in bearing the righteous judgment of God
against sin. This was the depth of the suffering of the
Lord Jesus, that which caused Him to cry out in the
thick darkness:

> My God, my God, why hast thou forsaken me? (Matt.
> 27:46).

It was from this that His holy soul shrank in the Garden
of Gethsemane, not from fear, but from very holiness.
Many brave men have borne great physical suffering un-
flinchingly, but only the sinless Son of God could bear
this suffering. To be made sin—how little we know of the
effect which that would have in the soul of a perfectly
sinless Person.

But the Lord Jesus could look on beyond the suffering. "For the joy that was set before him," that is, in ex-
change for that, He "endured the cross, despising the
shame, and is set down at the right hand of the throne of
God" (Heb. 12:2). All this Isaiah saw. He "shall see
his seed," he said. The Lord Jesus had in view that great
multitude of sons whom He was to bring into glory
(Heb. 2:10). When viewed in this light, the true light,

the death of Christ is not a tragedy, not a waste, but the greatest triumph possible. This is proved by the fact that death could not hold Him—"he shall prolong his days." The Old Testament in a number of passages foresees the resurrection of Christ, that other essential element of the Gospel.

> He shall see of the travail of his soul, and shall be satisfied.

How many times in human history men have dared to accomplish stupendous feats all for nothing. Not so with the Lord Jesus. Here is the crown of His atonement —"satisfied"! The question that comes to every individual who comes in contact with this truth is: "Are you satisfied?" To put it even more personally: "Am I satisfied with that which the Lord Jesus Christ did for me upon the cross?" By "his knowledge," that is, by the knowledge of Himself, God's "righteous servant" justifies. He can do this because He has already borne their iniquities. "By him all that believe," the Scripture says, "are justified from all things . . ." (Acts 13:39).

The prophecy closes with the same thought with which it began, exaltation after the suffering. In this brief passage we see both of the major themes of Old Testament prophecy in general: "the sufferings of Christ, and the glory that should follow" (I Peter 1:11). The spoils of this tremendous and unique campaign are now divided. The Messiah has come into His own. Psalm 2 and Psalm 72 are good examples of other prophetic Scriptures which speak of the coming day of Christ's triumph and millennial reign.

Is it possible to read a passage such as Isaiah 53 and to see it only as a dim and far-off event, something which had meaning to the prophet and the people of his own

day, but not to subsequent times? Alas, yes, for "the god
of this world [age] hath blinded the minds of them which
believe not, lest the light of the glorious gospel of Christ,
who is the image of God, should shine unto them" (II
Cor. 4:4) ! To the seeking heart, the believing heart, the
Lord Jesus is revealed in all the sad-joyous tragedy-
triumph of His substitutionary, sacrificial death and in
all the unalloyed joy and triumph of His glorious bodi-
ly resurrection. The Servant of Jehovah is the Christ
of Calvary and of the empty tomb.

CHAPTER 17

SALVATION THROUGH THE SERVANT

T HE CHAPTERS WHICH FOLLOW the climactic "Servant" passage (54–57) are directly related to it. We have already seen that the second part of Isaiah is divided into three sections of nine chapters each. This section speaks of the suffering Servant as the Redeemer. We have seen in chapter 53 how the redemption is accomplished. Here we see the application of that redemption to the nation of Israel and to the individual.

The Song of the Restored Wife

We must not lose sight of the fact that Isaiah tells of the comfort of God for Israel. We can be thankful that through faith in the Lord Jesus Christ, everyone of us now, whether Jew or Gentile, can enter in to the spiritual benefits of His death. This does not alter the fact, however, that God has made national promises to Israel. Here the nation is seen as a barren, desolate wife restored to fellowship and blessing (ch. 54) .

We can readily see that there is figurative language in a passage such as this. Israel is more than once compared to a wife. The principle which must be insisted upon, however, is that figurative language does not change the over-all literal fulfillment of prophecy. The most basic principle of Bible interpretation is at stake, and those who recklessly deny any future blessings for the nation of Israel have cast themselves adrift in a hopeless sea of allegorism, without chart or compass. If all the future blessings promised to the nation Israel are to be fulfilled spiritually in the Church, as many allege, why are not those same interpreters willing to take upon themselves all the curses pronounced upon the nation Israel?

Many Gentiles will undoubtedly be surprised and even chagrined to find that Israel is to have the leading place in the earth:

> For thou shalt break forth on the right hand and on the left; and thy seed shall inherit the Gentiles, and make the desolate cities to be inhabited (v. 3).

God has a relationship to Israel which He has never had and never will have to any other nation—"thy Maker is thine husband" (v. 5). Yet blessings will overflow from Israel to the whole earth. Israel's Redeemer is to be recognized as "The God of the whole earth" (v. 5). Paul speaks of this in his consideration of Israel's place in God's purpose:

> I say then, Have they stumbled that they should fall? God forbid: but rather through their fall salvation is come unto the Gentiles, for to provoke them to jealousy. Now if the fall of them be the riches of the world, and the diminishing of them the riches of the Gentiles; how much more their fullness? . . . For if the casting away of them be the reconciling of the world, what shall the receiving of them be, but life from the dead? (Rom. 11:11, 12, 15).

This passage in Isaiah, as well as many others, speaks of the "receiving" of Israel, its restoration to the place of blessing. It cannot help but affect the nations and the whole world.

Appeal to the Thirsty

Here again (ch. 55) is a well-known passage. God's Word is full of such gracious appeals. The only requisite for coming to God is a burning thirst (cf. John 7:37 and Rev. 22:17). This is no ordinary thirst, but the "hunger and thirst after righteousness," of which the Lord Jesus spoke (Matt. 5:6). In its context this appeal is addressed primarily to Israel, but in its application it is as broad as the human race. Everyone who seeks the Lord in the manner described here will find Him.

Is there any doubt that God's Word will be fulfilled? None whatever, is the assurance of God Himself: "It shall not return unto me void, but it shall accomplish that which I please, and it shall prosper in the thing whereto I sent it" (v. 11). All the glorious prophecies of blessings which flow from the suffering of the Servant will be fulfilled.

The passage closes with a poetic description of millennial joy. It may be compared with the song of salvation in chapter 12 as well as with certain of the millennial psalms.

Moral Exhortations in View of God's Salvation

Salvation always brings with it the responsibility of godly living. It is described here (ch. 56), of course, in an Old Testament setting of sabbath-keeping, but the principle is not hard to find. It is the principle of trust in God and of obedience to Him. True worship, even in the

Old Testament economy of ceremony and symbol, was a matter of the heart. The temple was primarily a "house of prayer" (v. 7). The Lord Jesus quoted from this verse when He cleansed the temple the second time:

> And said unto them, It is written, My house shall be called the house of prayer; but ye have made it a den of thieves (Matt. 21:13; cf. Mark 11:17; Luke 19:46).

Contrast of the Contrite and the Wicked

When God's salvation is made known to men, there are always those who accept it and those who reject it. There were those in Isaiah's day and afterward who would not be warned concerning the judgment that was to come in the captivity. They could not or would not understand that the righteous man who died was being "taken away from the evil to come" (57:1).

Isaiah contains, as we have seen, passages of transcendent beauty concerning the personality and majesty of God. They are transcendently beautiful because they are true and because they present God in His condescending grace:

> For thus saith the high and lofty One that inhabiteth eternity, whose name is Holy; I dwell in the high and holy place, with him also that is of a contrite and humble spirit, to revive the spirit of the humble, and to revive the heart of the contrite ones (v. 15).

Earthly sovereigns are thought of as dwelling with the exalted and proud ones; the great Sovereign of all dwells with the humble believer. This is a consolation and an encouragement to the trusting heart. There is danger, however, that the believer will fasten his thoughts on himself rather than upon God; then he loses his humility. A real glimpse of God, such as Isaiah has described from his own experience in chapter 6, will provoke contrition and humility.

The contrast to the contrite is described in the concluding verses.

> But the wicked are like the troubled sea, when it cannot rest, whose waters cast up mire and dirt (v. 20).

One might almost think that God is describing our day. Certainly there is increasing restlessness abroad in the earth. Men run here and there, seek satisfaction in this and that, try this panacea and that nostrum, but remain without peace and rest. One does not have to be a vile criminal in the eyes of men in order to fall into the classification described here. The contrast is between the contrite and the wicked. Consequently a man is either one or the other. The New Testament shows us that rejection of the Lord Jesus Christ is the most heinous and reprehensible of all sins:

> He that believeth on him is not condemned: but he that believeth not is condemned already, because he hath not believed in the name of the only begotten Son of God. . . . He that believeth on the Son hath everlasting life: and he that believeth not the Son shall not see life; but the wrath of God abideth on him (John 3:18, 36).

True peace of any kind can come only through the Lord Jesus Christ, the Redeemer, who has been prophetically described in this section. The section closes with the refrain echoed from the end of chapter 48:

> There is no peace, saith my God, to the wicked (v. 21).

CHAPTER 18

THE REDEEMER'S COMING
TO ZION

W$_E$ HAVE COME NOW to the last section of the second
part of Isaiah. It will perhaps be helpful to note
the structure of these concluding chapters in the setting
of the whole division and of the whole book.

ISAIAH—"THE SALVATION OF JEHOVAH"

Part One: The Judgment of God upon Israel (1—39)

Part Two: The Comfort of God for Israel (40—66)

  I. Deliverance of God's People (40-48)

  II. The Suffering Servant as the Redeemer (49—57)

  III. The Glorious Consummation (58—66)

    A. Repentance Followed by Blessing (58)

    B. The Coming of the Redeemer to Zion (59)

    C. The Glory of Israel (60)

    D. The Ministry of the Messiah (61)

    E. "Jerusalem a Praise in the Earth" (62)

    F. The Day of Vengeance (63)

    G. The Prayer of the Remnant (64)

    H. Condemnation and Glory (65)

    I. Peace Like a River (66)

Repentance Followed by Blessing

The closing section of the book describes the glorious consummation which God has in store for Israel, the people of the Servant, and God's channel of blessing to the world. There is a strong contrast throughout the section between the rebellious and the faithful, a contrast which is never entirely absent from any extended portion of the Word of God.

At the very beginning of Isaiah we saw that much of the worship of God was only formal or nominal. Here the lesson is repeated that the outward forms of repentance do not necessarily indicate a change of heart. Fasting, unaccompanied by the doing of right, is not sufficient:

> Is not this the fast that I have chosen? to loose the bands of wickedness, to undo the heavy burdens, and to let the oppressed go free, and that ye break every yoke? (58:6).

Such repentance will assure God's answer (v. 9). Delight in the Lord will cause His people to "ride upon the high places of the earth" (v. 14), to inherit that which God had promised the descendants of Jacob.

The Coming of the Redeemer to Zion

Chapter 59 continues in the same vein as the preceding chapter. What is it which causes the one who prays to feel that he is not heard? What is it which hinders the answer? It is sin. This is always true. The fault is not with God, but with the one who calls upon God. God is always ready to give the answer, to provide the deliverance. Since God could not find among the nation those who could be true intercessors, He provided salvation in

His sovereign grace and righteousness (v. 16). This leads to the same wonderful Person who has appeared in so many different ways in this incomparable prophecy of Isaiah, the Redeemer, the Lord Jesus Christ:

> And the Redeemer shall come to Zion, and unto them that turn from transgression in Jacob, saith the LORD (v. 20).

The Glory of Israel

The first three verses of chapter 60 show the coming of the light. This is reminiscent of chapter 9, and again refers to the Messiah. Paul uses the same sort of expression in II Corinthians 4:6 when he says:

> For God, who commanded the light to shine out of darkness, hath shined in our hearts, to give the light of the knowledge of the glory of God in the face of Jesus Christ.

The mention of the "glory of the LORD" carries one back in thought to chapter 40, where also it was mentioned that "the glory of the LORD shall be revealed." Here is the added thought that the light which comes upon Israel will attract the Gentiles.

The remainder of the chapter describes in some detail the homage which the Gentiles will pay to Israel. God's righteousness requires just retribution for the mistreatment accorded Israel in the past by many nations. Those who are in bondage to the terrible bias of anti-semitism will not like what God says here:

> For the nation and kingdom that will not serve thee shall perish; yea, those nations shall be utterly wasted. . . . The sons also of them that afflicted thee shall come bending unto thee; and all they that despised thee shall bow themselves down at the soles of thy feet; and they shall call thee, The city of the LORD, The Zion of the Holy One of Israel (vv. 12, 14).

Astonishing changes are in store for this earth—moral changes, political changes, economic changes. When God works His sovereign purpose, as described in these prophecies, Israel will be what God intended it to be— a witness to Himself in the earth. When Israel becomes what it is supposed to be, and when the Gentiles assume their appointed place in relation to Israel, then there will be righteousness and peace in the earth. All of this, however, depends upon a Person, the Person who speaks in the next chapter.

CHAPTER 19

THE MINISTRY OF THE MESSIAH

C HAPTERS 61–63 form the heart of this concluding section of Isaiah's prophecy. In chapter 61 the Messiah's ministry is described; in chapter 62 the result of that
ministry is seen in Israel's restoration; in chapter 63 the
day of vengeance is announced, and the prayer and praise
of the believing remnant of the nation are given.

The Words of the Anointed One

Sometimes in Isaiah it is hard to know who is speaking. Here at the beginning of the chapter (61) the
speaker tells us that He has been "anointed." This is the
root from which comes the term *Messiah* ("the anointed
One") . The word *anointed* is the clue and the New
Testament is the proof that the speaker here is none
other than the Lord Jesus Christ.

We see here, as in many other places in the prophets,
and as has been mentioned earlier, a blending together
of the two advents of the Lord Jesus Christ. The present
age between the advents, the age in which we are living,
is not the specific subject of Old Testament prophecy.
In fact, Peter tells us that the prophets themselves were
perplexed about the seeming contradictions in the predic-
tions concerning the "sufferings of Christ, and the glory

that should follow" (I Peter 1:11). From observing this we can learn to look for the proper distinctions in prophecy. We can see also how fulfilled prophecies set the pattern, so to speak, for those prophecies that are yet unfulfilled.

This is the passage from which the Lord Jesus Himself read in the synagogue at Nazareth, as recorded in Luke 4:16-31. In His reading, the Lord read only a part of the prophecy, stopping indeed in the middle of a sentence. The reason is obvious, for the Lord Jesus followed His reading by announcing, "This day is this scripture fulfilled in your ears" (Luke 4:21). He read only the part which was fulfilled that day; the remainder, having to do with the "day of vengeance of our God," was not being fulfilled at that time, and is even yet in the future, at our Lord's return.

"The Spirit of the Lord GOD is upon me . . ." Here are the three Persons of the Godhead mentioned together in the same brief clause. In connection with Isaiah's commission (ch. 6) we have already seen that the Old Testament contains numerous intimations of the doctrine of the Trinity, although the full exposition of the doctrine is reserved for the New Testament. Some of the great heroes of Old Testament times could say that the Spirit of God was upon them for the tasks to which God had called them, but none could say it in the same measure that this One could. The Lord Jesus Christ, the Son of God and Son of man, is the One who has been given the Holy Spirit in all His infinite fullness, for there was no hindrance of any kind at any time in His life.

> For he whom God hath sent speaketh the words of God: for God giveth not the Spirit by measure unto him (John 3:34).

"Because the LORD hath anointed me," He continues.
At the baptism of the Lord Jesus the Holy Spirit de-
scended upon Him. He is the Fulfiller of all types of
anointing in the Old Testament—the anointing of prophets, of priests, and of kings. He is The Anointed One, the
Messiah, the Christ.

As the Lord Jesus read these wonderful words from
Isaiah's prophecy and began to comment upon them, it
is no wonder that "the eyes of all them that were in the
synagogue were fastened on him" (Luke 4:20). Here
was something that could not happen often. Here was
a man definitely claiming to be the Messiah, so long
prophesied and so long awaited. There is no ambiguity
here; there could be no misunderstanding of what He
claimed. Suppose someone spoke in your church, read an
Old Testament prophecy, and claimed to be the fulfillment of it. Would this not be an occasion for astonishment? Yet there was something about this One who made
such claims which incited the admiration of even the
most grudging:

> And all bare him witness, and wondered at the gracious
> words which proceeded out of his mouth (Luke 4:22).

One might think that His words would have been received with joy and thanksgiving. As He went on, however, animosity and opposition increased, until finally
the people of Nazareth rose up in sinful wrath against
Him and actually tried to kill Him by casting Him over
a precipice. So it is in this world. Gracious words often
rouse only the guilty consciences of men and cause them
to want to do harm to the one who reminds them of their
sin.

The first three verses of the chapter tell of the mission
of Christ, and a wonderful mission it was. Here was One

who brought "good tidings." Here was One who proclaimed a far greater deliverance than any deliverance from Babylon or other earthly enemies; One who opened the prison house of sin and bade the poor prisoners come out into the glorious liberty of the children of God. Here was One who announced "the acceptable year of Jehovah," a long, gracious "year" which is even now continuing. But this same One will also bring "the day of vengeance of our God." There is no doubt significance in the relative use of these two terms; the word *year* is used for the time of grace, because it is God's good pleasure to extend it, that many may come to the Saviour; the word *day* is used for the time of judgment.

The words of the Lord Jesus concerning the fulfillment of this prophecy show the nearsightedness of those critics who insist that every prophecy must have an immediate fulfillment in the prophet's own time. The statement confirms the contention which was made earlier in our study that basically the issue is between the unbeliever and the Lord Jesus Christ Himself.

Verses 4-8 describe the benefits of the Messiah's mission upon Israel. The nation which God originally proposed to make a "kingdom of priests" (Exod. 19:6), after long failure truly will become so (v. 6).

Verse 9 indicates the effect of His mission upon the world. The chapter closes with the singing forth of the joy of the Lord.

"Jerusalem a Praise in the Earth"

The Jerusalem that is here described will have come a long way from the "Sodom" of chapter 1. This is Jerusalem as God wants it to be, as God will cause it to be,

"a crown of glory in the hand of the LORD" (v. 3). The
new names which God gives to the city and to the land
indicate the contrast to their former forsaken and desolate condition. *Hephzibah* means "my delight is in her,"
and *Beulah* means "married" (v. 4); the next verse
gives the explanation. God's very character is at stake,
so to speak, for He has promised by an oath that He will
restore Jerusalem. The "watchmen" are to remind God
continually of His Word and "give him no rest, till he
establish, and till he make Jerusalem a praise in the
earth" (v. 7).

God's Word must be fulfilled, and no amount of
spiritualizing or allegorizing can destroy the plain intent
of it. Jerusalem cannot mean here the heavenly Jerusalem, much less the church. This Jerusalem is to be
made a "praise in the earth." Here as so often in Isaiah
the wheel has completely turned—judgment is past and
comfort has come. The previously used expression, the
"highway," is used again to picture graphically the return of the people to Zion:

> Behold, the LORD hath proclaimed unto the end of the
> world, Say ye to the daughter of Zion, Behold, thy salva-
> tion cometh; behold, his reward is with him, and his work
> before him. And they shall call them, The holy people,
> The redeemed of the LORD: and thou shalt be called,
> Sought out, A city not forsaken (vv. 11, 12).

The Day of Vengeance

The next chapter (63) opens with a dialogue, or it
might almost be called in modern terminology an inter-
view. To the astonished question, "Who is this . . . ?"
the Messiah Himself answers:

> I that speak in righteousness, mighty to save (v. 1).

This is not a picture of the cross. It is true that the Lord Jesus suffered and died there alone, but this is a description of coming judgment. The blood which stains His garments in this picture is not His own blood, shed for us, but rather the blood of His enemies (v. 3). This is a graphic representation of "the day of vengeance" (v. 4). The "acceptable year" will be over by that time; the Saviour will have become the Judge. Some of the imagery in the Book of Revelation is drawn from this chapter, especially the mention of the wine press in chapter 14 and the description of the coming of the Lord Jesus Christ in judgment in chapter 19:

> And he was clothed with a vesture dipped in blood: and his name is called The Word of God (Rev. 19:13).

Prayer and Praise of the Godly Remnant

It is not incongruous to find this stern picture of judgment followed immediately by the mention of "the lovingkindnesses of the LORD" (v. 7). Some indeed would see only one side of the truth; misconstruing the love of God, they would deny or overlook His holiness. Right cannot triumph unless wrong is put down. And we live at present in a world of wrong. It *would be* most incongruous if the Saviour were *not* ultimately the Judge. In His judgment, furthermore, He is not harsh or arbitrary or cruel, but is still the longsuffering, merciful, gracious God. But grace spurned can only lead to judgment.

The judgment of evil-doers will result in deliverance for the oppressed people of God. Hence the song of God's lovingkindness. There is in these verses (7-19) a resumé of some of the history of Israel. There is an appeal to God to deliver as in the days of old. The deliverance from Egypt in the time of Moses is viewed as a parallel to this expected deliverance. There is the consciousness of belonging to God, which assures that He will work in mighty redemption.

CHAPTER 20

THE GLORIOUS CONSUMMATION

IN THE CLOSING CHAPTERS of Isaiah (64—66) there is a
mingling of condemnation and glory in a manner to
which the careful reader of the book has become ac-
customed. The great panorama of the second part of the
book sweeps before us in its portrayal of deliverance from
Babylon as a foretaste of an even greater deliverance; in
its description of the Messiah, the Servant of Jehovah,
through whom deliverance comes; and in its building
up to this climax of the glorious future for the nation
of Israel. All the blessing is through the Servant, who
is also the Avenger, the Executor of the wrath of God.
Chapter 64 continues the aspirations of the godly remnant of Israel; chapter 65 contains the answer of Jehovah to their prayer; and the concluding chapter (66)
describes God's final judgments in the restoration of
Israel and vengeance upon the transgressors. There is
no suspense in this story for one who follows it from the
beginning; the end is fully known, but each time the
story is retold, each time the dominant themes are repeated, there is a new impact upon the soul.

Prayer for the Manifestation of God's Presence

The godly remnant of the nation, acutely aware of

117

God's almighty power in the past history of the nation, express their earnest longing for a repetition in their own time:

> Oh that thou wouldest rend the heavens, that thou wouldest come down . . . (64:1).

Those who pray know that God is able and that the things of God are far beyond human experience and understanding. Paul makes use of the thought of verse 4 in I Corinthians:

> But as it is written, Eye hath not seen, nor ear heard, neither have entered into the heart of man, the things which God hath prepared for them that love him (I Cor. 2:9).

Does this mean that we can never know these things? Not at all:

> But God hath revealed them unto us by his Spirit: for the Spirit searcheth all things, yea, the deep things of God (I Cor. 2:10).

As always the godly identify themselves with the nation at large, and confess sin to God. They acknowledge that God's judgments have come because of sin (v. 5).

> But we are all as an unclean thing, and all our righteousnesses are as filthy rags; and we all do fade as a leaf; and our iniquities, like the wind, have taken us away (v. 6).

Somehow those who know God best are most conscious of their own sinfulness. Isaiah himself found this so, as we have seen in chapter 6. Find a man who is self-sufficient, who has no awareness of sin, and you find a man lost and undone and bound for Hell. These who confess their sin in the prophecy know that they cannot base their appeal to God on any merit of their own. They realize that they have no merit. Even their "righteousnesses" are worthless in God's sight; "filthy rags," to be cast aside. On what then can they base their appeal? On the only ground that anyone can ever find in any dispensation under any circumstances—on the mercy and grace of God.

> But now, O LORD, thou art our father; we are the clay, and thou our potter; and we all are the work of thy hand. Be not wroth very sore, O LORD, neither remember iniquity forever: behold, see, we beseech thee, we are all thy people (vv. 8, 9).

Jehovah's Reply

In His reply (ch. 65) God brings out the fact of the rebelliousness of the nation of Israel. The description of them here is reminiscent of the very first chapter of the prophecy. God reiterates His purpose to recompense their rebelliousness. One of the worst features of their sinful attitude is their self-righteousness, self-deceptive and hypocritical—"holier than thou" (v. 5).

The Holy Spirit's application of the opening verses of this chapter in the New Testament is instructive:

> But Esaias [Isaiah] is very bold, and saith, I was found of them that sought me not; I was made manifest unto them that asked not after me. But to Israel he saith, All day long have I stretched forth my hands unto a disobedient and gainsaying people (Rom. 10:20, 21).

Yet as the New Testament application goes on to show, this does not mean that God has cast away His people (Rom. 11:1-6). There is always the remnant, the true Israel, the godly "tenth" that "shall return" (Isa. 6:13). This remnant is in view in verses 8-10. God will not "destroy them all," but will "bring forth a seed" to inherit the promises. The succeeding verses paint the contrast of condemnation and glory. God, addressing the rebellious and ungodly, shows how their judgment is in contrast to the blessings upon His servants:

> Thus saith the Lord GOD, Behold, my servants shall eat, but ye shall be hungry: behold, my servants shall drink, but ye shall be thirsty: behold, my servants shall rejoice, but ye shall be ashamed: behold, my servants shall sing for joy of heart, but ye shall cry for sorrow of heart, and shall howl for vexation of spirit (vv. 13, 14).

The chapter closes with further description of kingdom blessings. The last verse carries one back in thought to the similar description of the Millennium in chapter 11. It will be a glorious day when these words are fulfilled:

> They shall not hurt nor destroy in all my holy mountain, saith the LORD (v. 25).

As in chapter 2 and elsewhere the "mountain" refers to God's kingdom, and the various references to it show that it will be a universal kingdom. Daniel, carrying out the same thought, speaks of the stone which "became a great mountain, and filled the whole earth" (Dan. 2:35).

God's Final Judgments

The opening verses of chapter 66 are quoted by Stephen in his address before the Jewish council, as recorded in Acts 7:49, 50, to bring out the truth of God's omnipresence. He cannot be contained in any building, no matter how magnificent. Solomon realized this when he dedicated the temple to God (I Kings 8:27; II Chron. 2:6; 6:18). The ungodly are warned that because of their continuance in sin their very sacrifices to God at the temple are sinful.

Nevertheless, Jerusalem will yet rejoice. God "will extend peace to her like a river" (v. 12). Israel will be restored from the far places in which it has been scattered (v. 20) and the transgressors will receive their due (v. 24). The solemn ending of the book reminds us again that when unrighteousness is rampant, God can bring in righteousness only by severe and searching judgment. The Lord Jesus makes use of the expressions from this verse to describe the agony of the lost:

> Where their worm dieth not, and the fire is not quenched (Mark 9:44).

While the emphasis in the prophecy is upon the establishment of the millennial kingdom, there is a brief glimpse of "the new heavens and the new earth" (v. 22), more fully viewed in the New Testament:

> And I saw a new heaven and a new earth: for the first heaven and the first earth were passed away; and there was no more sea (Rev. 21:1).

CHAPTER 21

RETROSPECT

EACH PERSON who reads and studies the Book of Isaiah will doubtless have many impressions of his own about this wonderful book. Certain impressions, however, will be common to a great many readers. One of these is the magnitude of the prophecy. There is so much here in time and range of ideas that even one who is fairly familiar with the book will frequently have a sense of being overwhelmed. This is to be expected, for Isaiah did not originate this prophecy. He "spake" as he was "moved by the Holy Ghost" (II Peter 1:21). If the Word of God were thoroughly comprehensible at a glance, it would not be the Word of God. Its scope and depth are proofs that it truly is from God.

It is quite possible, however, even from an elementary study such as this to get a grasp of the book as a whole and to "think through" it, at least in general terms. Its basic outline, as has been shown, is not difficult. A mastery of the sections of the outline should be of help in remembering the contents of the book. Thinking back over the outline which has been followed, it can be seen that the Book of Isaiah is in two main divisions, the former consisting of seven sections and the latter of three. Whatever titles are used, the contents of the sections stand out in any reading of the book:

Part One: The Judgment of God (1—39)
   I. Opening Prophecies (1—6)
  II. Prophecies of Immanuel (7—12)
 III. The Burdens (13—23)
 IV. Punishment and Kingdom Blessing (24—27)
   V. The Woes (28—33)
 VI. Indignation and Glory (34, 35)
VII. Historical Interlude (36—39)

Part Two: The Comfort of God (40—66)
  I. Deliverance of God's People (40—48)
 II. The Suffering Servant as the Redeemer **(49—57)**
III. The Glorious Consummation (58—66)

One cannot stress too much the necessity of reading and meditating upon the Book of Isaiah itself. This is especially true because the Word of God is not like any merely human book. There is a spiritual as well as an intellectual element in the apprehension of it. One could know the various sections of the book perfectly and could even think through it by chapters without entering into its spiritual teaching. Therefore, we must always avoid mere knowledge for the sake of knowledge, but must allow the Spirit of God to make personal application of the Word to our own lives.

It is useless to trace the judgment of God in Isaiah and to note His comfort for His people if one sees it all as an abstraction, as a beautiful but theoretical essay or story. God's Word is intensely practical, and if we cannot learn from both its precepts and its examples, there is something wrong with us as individuals. We must not become so absorbed in the beauties of style and the symmetrical

arrangement of Isaiah that we lose sight of our own need
of repentance and trust in the Redeemer depicted there.

A second impression which may be gained from the
reading of Isaiah is the reality of the promised kingdom
for the nation of Israel. In the face of so large a body
of prophecy concerning future blessings for the despised
and scattered nation, it is hard to see how so many
readers and interpreters blithely assume that the Church
is everywhere in view, that the Church is Israel, that the
Church is the kingdom, and that there is no objective
standard in the fulfillment of prophecy. It is because
of this prevalent misconception that so much stress has
been placed in the present survey upon the literal fulfillment of prophecy.

Another impression from the Book of Isaiah is the
realization of the majesty and greatness of God. As has
been mentioned before, the God who is described in the
Book of Isaiah, in His omniscience, His omnipotence,
His omnipresence, His eternity, His immutability, His
holiness, His love, His mercy, and His grace cannot by
any stretch of the imagination be brought down to the
level of the rationalistic, destructive critics. To speak of
the God of the Old Testament as a "tribal" or "national"
God is sheer nonsense, and it is equally nonsensical to
suppose that the godly people of Old Testament times
thought of God in that way. As has been seen clearly,
Isaiah's message is a universal message, reaching to the
"ends of the earth."

Perhaps too little stress has been placed in this study
upon the particular characterization of God which is
afforded by Isaiah's favorite title, "The Holy One of
Israel." God is not the God of mere naked power, but
the God of holiness. His nature is always in perfect

harmony with His moral character. All that He is and
all that He does is right, absolutely pure, absolutely
free from all defilement of sin. Because He is the Holy
One, He can redeem those who put their trust in Him,
and He must judge and punish those who reject and
disobey Him.

Along with his description of God's glory and majesty
and his delineation of God as the Holy One, Isaiah does
not neglect that aspect of God's character which is comprehended in the term, the love of God. His goodness,
His longsuffering, His mercy, His grace, His gentleness,
His lovingkindness—all these are seen in abundant measure in the pages of this book.

These are more or less random impressions—impressions of the magnitude of the book itself, of the promised
future for the nation of Israel, of the nature and character of God—yet as indicated above they are probably
impressions common to a great many readers of the
book. There is still another outstanding impression
which must be mentioned and emphasized, even though
notice was taken of it at the beginning of our study.
That is the Messianic character of the Book of Isaiah.

If you have faithfully read Isaiah and have made some
use of the comments set down in this survey, you surely
can no longer wonder why Isaiah is spoken of as the
"prophet of the gospel" or the "evangelical prophet."
One could reconstruct a fairly detailed account of the
earthly life and ministry, the death and resurrection of
our Lord from the pages of Isaiah alone. We have seen
that the Messianic references are not confined to one
section of the book, but are scattered all through it. The
Person of Christ is here—His absolute deity, His perfect
humanity, His incarnation through the virgin birth,

His lowly manner of life. His compassionate teaching
and miracles, His substitutionary death for us, His resurrection, His glorification, His place as the Judge of all.

Yet we must not make the same mistake that the religious leaders of Christ's day made. They looked for
eternal life in the bare pages of Scripture and rejected the
Person whom those pages described. He said to them:

> Ye search the scriptures, for in them ye think ye have
> eternal life; and these are they which bear witness of me;
> and ye will not come unto me that ye might have life
> (John 5:39, 40, A.S.V.).

It is not enough to marvel at the prophetic pictures
of Christ in Isaiah, pictures so sharply drawn that they
could not be accidental. One must have a personal relationship to the Christ there described. The Gospel is
here in its pure essence, given prophetically by the Holy
Spirit long before the Lord Jesus actually came into the
world. Isaiah saw His glory, and we can see His glory too
in Isaiah's prophecy. Will our response be that of the
prophet himself? God grant it may be so.

The tragedy of Israel's unbelief is set forth in all its
stark reality at the close of the Book of Acts, and, as
might be expected, it is set forth by a quotation from
Isaiah.

The apostle Paul, following his customary procedure of
giving the Jews an opportunity to accept Christ when-
ever he came to a new locality, spoke at length with the
Jewish men of influence who would come to his house
in Rome. "From morning till evening" he discussed with
them the Scriptures concerning Christ (Acts 28:23).
The record tells us that he expounded the law of Moses
and the prophets, and we can be very sure that Isaiah
was referred to a great many times in the course of that

momentous discussion. The results, from a human point of view, were disappointing:

> And some believed the things which were spoken, and some believed not. And when they agreed not among themselves, they departed, after that Paul had spoken one word, Well spake the Holy Ghost by Esaias [Isaiah] the prophet unto our fathers, saying, Go unto this people, and say, Hearing ye shall hear, and shall not understand; and seeing ye shall see, and not perceive: for the heart of this people is waxed gross, and their ears are dull of hearing, and their eyes have they closed; lest they should see with their eyes, and hear with their ears, and understand with their heart, and should be converted, and I should heal them. Be it known therefore unto you, that the salvation of God is sent unto the Gentiles, and that they will hear it (Acts 28: 24-28).

"The salvation of God"—"the salvation of Jehovah"—that is the theme of this prophecy, of which the prophet's name is the symbolic testimony. In accordance with the prophecy the message has gone out to the Gentiles; the message of Christ is being proclaimed to "the ends of the earth."

Moody Press, a ministry of the Moody Bible Institute, is designed for education, evangelization and edification. If we may assist you in knowing more about Christ and the Christian life, please write us without obligation to:

Moody Press, c/o MLM, Chicago, Illinois 60610.